Sweet Moments

INSIGHT AND ENCOURAGEMENT FOR THE PASTOR'S WIFE

Endorsements

Shelley Pierce's book is a delightful read. For pastors' wives this will be an entertaining, helpful and spiritually profitable book. I encourage all wives of God's men to get it!
—**Jerry Vines**, Pastor-Emeritus, First Baptist Church, Jacksonville, Florida; Twice President, Southern Baptist Convention.

Sweet Moments stirred up so many memories and took me right back to the emotions I felt at the time! Shelley truly understands this unique calling we are in as she has walked this path for many years ... I pray you all find comfort and companionship in these pages as I did!
—Kelly Noland

Sweet Moments brought back dozens of memories and the full range of emotions. Shelley understands that our unique calling can only truly be understood by others who have walked the same path. No matter what your path may be strewn with at the moment, you will find encouragement and companionship in these pages.
—Rhonda Van Cleave

After serving alongside my precious husband as a pastor's wife for over forty years, the Lord took him home. I'm left with wonderful memories of God's constant provision and blessing, but also, of challenges we faced along the way. In those times, I felt a loneliness that I could not share with anyone. *Sweet Moments* is a refreshing reminder that we do not serve alone but, as called women of God, who should support each other in good times and bad.
—George Ann Alexander

Wow! I'm so excited about this book! What a great resource for pastor's wives both young and old. Knowing that it doesn't matter what season of life you're in, there is someone that can understand it and help you along the way. It's a great thing. There aren't enough books like this one out there. A must have for any pastor's wife in need of encouragement. Which is all of us, right?
—Jennifer Hutchens

Wow! What an encouragement to all Pastor's wives who are in the daily grind of trying to balance family demands and ministry struggles! In her book, *Sweet Moments,* Shelley Pierce offers practical tips and wise counsel in various situations we find ourselves.
—Janae Persinger

Sweet Moments will certainly encourage the minister's spouse, as well as the minister. Unfortunately, ministry is oftentimes a place where the pastoral team feels ostracized, with no one whom they can fully open up to or trust. The sense of isolation leaves them vulnerable to feelings of discouragement or even defeat. This work is both heartening and inspiring.
—Loretta Goericke, M.Ed., Co-Pastor and Christian School Administrator

I remember sitting beside my husband in a Christmas program service as the choir sang about trusting the faithfulness of God, even in the struggles. Tears were streaming down my face because I knew that trust was hard in the moment. I tried to hide the tears from the youth sitting around us, but I knew God was speaking truth in my heart. *Sweet Moments* reminds me I don't have to have it all together as the pastor's wife. I still need to be real and grow in my relationship with Christ. God is faithful, but sometimes it can be hard to see that.
—Emily Fox

Sweet Moments

INSIGHT AND ENCOURAGEMENT FOR THE PASTOR'S WIFE

SHELLEY PIERCE

Cover and Interior Design: Derinda Babcock

Editor(s): Cristel Phelps, Deb Haggerty

Author Represented by Hartline Literary Agency

PUBLISHED BY: Elk Lake Publishing, Inc., 35 Dogwood Dr., Plymouth, MA 02360, 2019

Library Cataloging Data

Names: Pierce, Shelley (Shelley Pierce)

Sweet Moments: Insight and Encouragement for the Pastor's Wife / Shelley Pierce

180p. 23cm × 15cm (9in × 6 in.)

Description: Life as a pastor's wife has been a lot of fun, filled with new friendships and many learning opportunities. This life has also brought much heartache. I suppose we could say it is the best of times, it is the worst of times.

Identifiers: ISBN-13: 978-1-950051-13-7 (trade) | 978-1-950051-14-4 (POD) | 978-1-950051-15-1 (e-book.)

Key Words: Inspiration, Reinforcement, Support, Ministry, Understanding, Pastors, Family

LCCN: 2019933755 Nonfiction

Dedication

To Hilda Rhea Speights Pierce, my wonderful and kind mother-in-law. She modeled grace and tender care for the Bride of Christ. She taught me how to walk this path with grace and a grateful heart. Pastor's wife for over sixty-five years, she shows me Jesus.

Acknowledgments

Thank you Cyle Young, Bethany Morehead, and Hartline Literary Agency; Deb Haggerty and Elk Lake Publishing, Inc.; editor Cristel Phelps and graphic designer Derinda Babcock—I thank God for you. God blessed me beyond measure when he placed me on your team.

The countless women in ministry who faithfully and selflessly serve.

My children, James, Hannah, John, and Abigail. All grown and with families of their own, I see God's mercy and grace in them. They survived the glass house!

And my husband, James K. "Tommy" Pierce, who honored me with this title by making me his wife. Thank you for always being an example of Christ and speaking truth in my life.

Welcome!

I think of you as a friend, and the words that follow are more of a conversation over time. Maybe we can share a cup of coffee and a porch swing, sweet iced tea and the sound of ocean waves, or perhaps hot cocoa in front of a friendly fire.

The idea for *Sweet Moments* began many years ago. My sister called with a few questions. She wanted to understand and befriend her pastor's wife. This pastor's wife was young, had several children, and her husband entered the ministry well into their marriage. I made a joke that what she really needed was a big slice of cheesecake, and maybe I should write a book to encourage women in her shoes. My sister replied, "Do it! Do it! Do it!" You might say she poured water all over the seeds that were already planted.

Life as a pastor's wife has been a lot of fun, filled with new friendships and many learning opportunities. This life has also brought much heartache. I suppose we could say, to paraphrase Dickens, it is the best of times; it is the worst of times.

With each lesson learned, I have thought of you, wondered—are you all alone and longing for a friend? Are you earlobe deep in ministry and wondering where your joy went? Are you enjoying this unique calling? Do you know how very special you are to God?

I'm excited about our time together. Whether you are searching for where you belong or are in a wonderfully content place, let's use every experience to become more like Jesus.

I am aware I am not an expert on much. In fact, I have no doubt you could have written your own chapter. My prayer is that God will use these words to bring you comfort and strength and to draw you closer to him.

Every marriage is unique. Tommy and I have what might be referred to as a traditional pastor's family. He's the preacher; I am his wife and helper. Your marriage and ministry might be one of co-pastoring, or perhaps, you and your husband are missionaries. You will find two foundational truths in the following pages: the need to grow in Jesus, and the willingness to keep a conversation going with your spouse. Growing, talking, and listening is the only way this journey in ministry and life will be what God intends for you. God's plan is for us to thrive together.

In dealing with true-to-life issues, my intention is never to give the Bride of Christ a black eye. I love the church. To serve her this way is an honor and privilege. That said, you and I know there are people within the church who are hurtful. We can't pretend a fairytale reality.

Deep in my heart, I want to encourage you to faithfulness and joy as you live the life of the pastor's wife. I am cheering you on to laugh in between the difficult days. I hope you know just how great the Father's love is for you. And most of all, my prayer is through every part of this calling, you will grow closer to him.

Remember, as my momma reminded me, he is faithful to complete that which he started.

—Shelley

PS—The recipes tucked in this book are Pierce family favorites. They are yummy comfort treats shared by family members and friends in ministry, I hope you will try them and enjoy!

Contents

The Sisterhood of the Traveling Hearts: We're All on the Same Team xvii

1. Generations Apart: Joined at the Heart
A highlight of differences in the generations of pastor's wives with the focus on what we have in common. **1**

2.Help a Sister Out: What's Next for Me?
A special word of encouragement for new members of the sisterhood. **5**

Keep the Home Fires Burning: Choosing Only the Finest Ingredients for Living
God made you the heart of your home. Cherish it. Relish in it. Protect it. **9**

My Favorite Cake 10

3. The Beautiful Way We Love
Oftentimes, I feel like a mom to the people God has given us. **11**

4. Lipstick on His Collar: Graciously Sharing Your Husband
The pastor is every woman's spiritual leader, brother, or child. Learning to share him and be the gatekeeper at the same time is an art. **15**

5. Oh No, You Didn't! Drawing the Line in the Sand
Beware of the woman who does not see the pastor as a spiritual leader, brother, or child. Listening to your God-given instincts and handling the situation properly. **19**

6. Excuse Me, Dear, Didn't You Mean ...: Correcting Your Husband in Public
There is a time and a place for everything. **23**

7. He is Not Yours Alone: Your Husband's Absence on Christmas Day
Death doesn't take a vacation. Sometimes you need to be creative with your family time. **27**

Lemon Supreme Special Cake 31

8. Your Kids Are Like Eli's Sons: Protecting and Teaching Your Kids Under Attack
Biblical guidance for your children when they are guilty and when they are falsely accused. **33**

9. Ministry Isn't for Sissies: Weathering the Storms
What should you do when you don't know what to do? **37**

10. The Struggle is Real: Supporting Him on Mondays
Many of the most powerfully used pastors throughout history suffered from depression. Praying your husband through the down days. **41**

Wolves Among Us: Self-Control and Bites of Sweet Freedom 45

Connie Faulkner Pie 46

11. If I Had Known Then: Well, You Couldn't Have Known Then, So Stop That
The biblical response to regrets and the future. **47**

12. Wolves in Sheep's Clothing: Those Who Seek to Hurt
David turned to God for protection and wisdom. You can too. **51**

13. Please Pray for Me: Praying for Others While Your Own Heart is Breaking
Your strength to help others during your own time of need comes from God. Practical tips for trusting him. **55**

14. He Didn't Speak to Me in the Hall: Smoothing Out the Speed Bumps
That awkward moment when you try to explain your husband's single focus on Sunday mornings. **59**

15. He Said What? From Your Lips to Their Ears
Remembering what you say carries weight. **63**

Banana Cream Pie 66

16. I'm Only Human: Seeking Forgiveness for Failure
The Biblical answer to messing up. **67**

17. The Church Is Messy
Remembering heaven is the only place that doesn't get messy. **73**

18. Checkmate: Remembering the True Enemy
People are not your enemy. Relying on the Bible through the battles. 77

Your Life is My Business: They Don't Own you 81

Best Sugar Cookies Ever 83

19. She's Putting on Weight: Yes, You Can Learn to Smile at What They Say
Responding in a kind manner to those who are thoughtless. **85**

20. I Cannot Be Your Friend: There's a Reason You Are Lonely
Choose your friends wisely. **89**

21. I Always Feel Like Somebody's Watching Me: Well, That's Because They Are
You are an example to others whether you like it or not. Make the best of the opportunities. **93**

22. My First Friend: Honest Above All
It takes years to build this kind of friendship. **97**

23. Monkey in the Middle: Ministering to The Hatfields and McCoys
The difficult task of being the pastor's wife to all people during conflict. **101**

24. Is It Well with My Soul?
Remembering God is faithful. **105**

Saving the Best Slice for the End of the Day:
Remembering Who You Are and Whose You Are 109

Pumpkin Cookies 110

25. Shouldn't You Know How to Play the Piano?
Breaking the mold and being who God created you to be. **111**

26. Who Am I: Losing Track of Your Purpose
When you are busy living up to the expectations of others, you forget the only One who matters. **115**

27. These Boots Were Made for Walkin'
Your congregation doesn't walk in your shoes, and it's okay. **119**

28. To Dream the Possible Dream: Dusting Off the Gifts God Gave You
Using your unique gifts to the glory of God. **127**

29. The Desperate Call: Help! I'm on Hold!
What happens when you call a pastor's family hotline, and they put you on hold? It could happen! **127**

Grandma Nellie's Peach Cobbler 131

30. Lord, I Believe! Help My Unbelief!
When you reach a faith crisis. **133**

31. Sit a Spell: Time at the Feet of Jesus
Keeping first things first. **137**

Granny's Banana Bread 141

32. The Child of the King: Garments of White Awaiting
The Scriptures are clear—the crown of life is given to those who overcome. You can do it! **143**

33. Build Your House on the Lord Jesus Christ.
Getting the foundation right. **147**

34. The Last Word: Be of Good Cheer
This gift of First Lady is a grand opportunity to serve God exceptionally. Embrace it and lean on God. He's all you need. **151**

It's Just Beginning ... 155

No Bake Chocolate Peanut Butter Cookies 156

Endnotes 157

About the Author 161

The Sisterhood of the Traveling Hearts: We're All on the Same Team

She sits quietly on the front row, hands folded and resting on her open Bible on her lap. She wears a long skirt. Her long hair carefully coiffed in a bun.

She wears flats and blue jeans. She hasn't been in worship in weeks … or has it been months? She rocks the babies, teaches the toddlers, and leads in children's worship. She organizes dinner-on-the-grounds the third Sunday of each month.

Her children follow quietly as they line up one by one in the second pew on the right. She has cautioned them to behave. There's a knot in her stomach caused by the fear that perhaps her knee-length dress is too short, or her blush is a tad too dark.

Methodist, Presbyterian, Southern Baptist, nondenominational or multidenominational—we need to focus on what we have in common.

We love Jesus, our husband, and our children. We struggle to find where we fit in. We are lonely. We wish folks weren't so critical. We rejoice and thank God for unexpected blessings. We desire to make a difference. We don't understand people. Oftentimes, we don't understand God. We are able to place the I-have-it-all-together expression believably on our face no matter what is going on in our heart.

We are so much alike we could wear team jerseys. We need each other.

Chapter One

Generations Apart: Joined at the Heart

A highlight of differences in the generations of pastors' wives with the focus on what we have in common.

> Only conduct yourselves in a manner worthy of the gospel of Christ, so that whether I come and see you or remain absent, I will hear of you that you are standing firm in one spirit, with one mind striving together for the faith of the gospel. (Philippians 1:27)

"Ladies, be sure you lay his socks out on Saturday. And be sure they match his suit. Now listen, don't buy him ankle socks. His socks need to go all the way to his knees. Nobody wants to see his white, hairy legs when he sits down on the platform."

These were the wise words of Mrs. Shirley Lindsey, first lady of First Baptist Church, Jacksonville, Florida, for thirty-one years. Homer knew he was one blessed man.

I was most fortunate to hear her teach at one of the pastors' conferences FBC held each year. What a treasure she was!

When I married Tommy in 1981, he wore crisply pressed, white dress shirts and beautiful suits. He polished his shoes every Saturday night just as his preacher-father had before him. I hold a vision in my heart of our firstborn son, in his sweet footed PJs, helping his daddy shine the shoes.

You know where this is going, I'm sure. Today's Sunday morning best is open-collared polos and blue jeans. Many preachers don't sit on the platform any longer because … well … there is no platform. To quote Tommy, "The message doesn't change—our mode of delivering it must."

The ties that bind us together are woven cords of God's grace when we mess up, God's strength when we are at our weakest, God's mercy when we are at a loss, and God's presence that whispers "you are never alone."

Most of us married into this life knowing our sweetheart's call into ministry. There are some of you out there, however, that have been surprised by the call. You married an engineer, a dentist, or a mechanic. News flash—none of us knew what we were getting ourselves into.

Let's stick together! There is most certainly strength in numbers, and when we pray for each other, we can trust God will do amazing things in our lives.

Several years ago, I was privileged to attend a pastors' wives retreat. With only a dozen or so in attendance, the retreat was a safe place to let down our guard. I arrived carrying my own baggage. Fresh on the heels of a church split, I was worn. I sat in sorrow-filled amazement as I listened to the heart cry of these women—more than one generation represented—all in great need of hope and help. One young mother wept as she related begging her husband to choose another profession. Anything but this! The church is the Bride of Christ. She is special and should be valued and nurtured and protected. Sadly, we often find ourselves serving in churches filled with people who either never knew the Lord or have forgotten our common calling. It's vital for us to talk to each other in a way that brings healing and not a black eye to the Bride.

Many of you are doing well to keep your head above water, that flood of discouragement that comes from constant criticism. We all fight the same enemy. The enemy is not the people. Our enemy is Satan alone. Let us pray for one another and rely on each other to be a safe place.

Those of us in the trenches know that reaching our communities with the Gospel grows increasingly difficult. We also know our differences—whether we sing from the hymnal or join our voices in choruses projected on a screen—do not separate us. We are on the same team.

And listen, ladies, whether your husband is twenty-three or eighty-three, Mrs. Lindsey was right. No one wants to see his hairy legs.

Father, I am grateful for the privilege of being my husband's support and best friend. Honestly, though, I am often afraid and tired. Place in me a heart of steadfast commitment to you; a heart of compassion for the people you have given me to serve;

and a heart of understanding for one another. Thank you for your promise to continue the work you began in me. With your strength, I know I can stand firm with my sisters in ministry with One Spirit.

Sweet bites of wisdom: "Be yourself. All that you are in Christ is edifying. Ann Lindberg said, 'Birds don't swim, and fish don't climb trees, and with God's help, I will make the most of my assets.' Our personalities and temperaments are unique." **—Janet Vines**[1]

Pick up your fork: Read Psalm 133 and John 17:20-26

Psalm 133

David tells us unity is pleasant. When my kids were in elementary school, they often played together in unity. Playtime was marked by a calm kind of joy. Now, disunity—loud and clamorous. No wonder David describes getting along as a pleasant thing!

What are the two comparisons David makes in verses two and three?

Fine oil was uncommon and exceptional. Compare unity among the first ladies in your community to fine oil being poured out. How would it impact you personally? How would this kind of unity impact the community for Christ?

Mount Hermon is in the north, and the hills of Zion are in the south. Imagine the sweet, silent dew from the snow-covered mountain as it whispers to the parched dry hills. This kind of unity brings life. How would a new friendship with women of like purpose bring life to you? Are you open to a new friendship?

John 17: 20-26

Jesus prayed for future believers to have unity. He knew local church families would compete with one another, swap disgruntled members, and compare missions offerings.

What difference would it make if we dropped the false faces, skipped the jealousies, and tossed out competition between churches?

Would your community see a difference?

How do David's song and Jesus's prayer challenge you today? What can you do to get the ball rolling?

Chapter 2

Help a Sister Out: What's Next for Me?

A special word of encouragement for new members of the sisterhood.

> ... not by way of eye service, as men-pleasers, but as slaves of Christ, doing the will of God from the heart. With good will render service, as to the Lord, and not to men, knowing that whatever good thing each one does, this he will receive back from the Lord, whether slave or free.
> Ephesians 6:6-8

She stood before me with wide eyes and an open heart. She would soon marry the love of her life. She had one question of me: "What advice will you give me before I marry into the ministry?"

Run!

Of course, I didn't say that. Truth be told, I wanted to cry for her. Young and in love and clueless as to the days and years ahead. Instead of telling her to run like the wind, I gave her the best biblical advice possible.

"Get up every morning with the goal to please Jesus. If you have prayed and studied the Bible, you will know what he requires of you. If someone in your church family is unhappy with you, you don't need to worry if you have lived to please God."

No matter what a person does for a living, they soon discover it's impossible to please all people. The job description for the pastor's wife changes with each parishioner.

We are viewed through the lens of past experience. If Sister Susan remembers a sweet and godly pastor's wife as she was growing up in the church, you will be viewed as kind and godly. However, if Unsure Ursula was somehow mistreated by the wife of a pastor, she will be slow to trust you.

We have a choice to make. We can strive to bake the best pie, keep our children from tripping up, wear the perfect length skirts and be all things to all people. Or, we can choose to wake up each morning and before our feet even touch the floor, talk to God and tell him we desire to please him and him alone.

We all have that one church member who seems to enjoy inflicting pain on our husband or family. Have you experienced a Sunday morning when you wished one of the children would wake with a low-grade temp so you could stay home from church? I have. I had those moments of thinking I could not possibly walk down the hall and hold my head up. It was when I came to the place of total reliance on God alone to meet me and fix me that I was able to look people in the eye and not fear what might be said. I learned the meaning of "the joy of the Lord is my strength."

There is freedom in choosing to please and honor God and God alone. We step off the treadmill of make-the-church-family-love-me. We can live the will of God from the heart and enjoy this unique position he has given us.

This wonderful, crazy, busy, painful, incredible, challenging, amazing, impossible life as the first lady is near to the heart of God. He has a plan to use our lives to touch the lives of others for his glory.

Don't run. Embrace who you are in Christ.

> *To the One who knows all things, I admit I am often scared to death. I fear messing up. I fear not being "enough." I fear I will say the wrong thing at the wrong time. And I am tired. I recognize I need you to protect me from myself and to keep me centered in doing your will.*
>
> *I want to walk in your strength. Help me to pray for those who hurt me and love those I cannot trust.*
>
> *Please keep me mindful of your love. Keep me aware of the choice to live to please you alone. I love you, Father. Oh, how I love you!*

Sweet bites of wisdom: "Pray for wisdom to know when to speak, what to say, and when to be "mum." Then when struggles come (and they will), face them with courage and confidence."

—June Bodenhamer[2]

Pick up your fork: Read Colossians 3 and Philippians 4:13, 19

Colossians 3

Colossians chapter three is packed. Paul gives instruction for us to know what to "take off" and what to "put on." Reread the chapter. Take the passage personally. What do you need to take off?

When you choose to "put on" kindness, compassion, and patience, everything in your life will change. Meditate on how Jesus wants to help you be more like him.

How do these changes influence your husband, children, friends, and church family?

How do these changes make your love relationship with Jesus stronger?

Philippians 4:13, 19

Philippians 4:13 and 19 remind us how Colossians 3 can be reached. We are experts at being self-sufficient. Are you trying to make these changes in your own strength? Why are you struggling? His intent is for us to do this first with his power and then together.

What are some concrete ways you can apply Philippians to Colossians?

Keep the Home Fires Burning: Choosing Only the Finest Ingredients for Living

God made you the heart of your home. Cherish it. Relish in it. Protect it.

> But the lovingkindness of the Lord is from everlasting to everlasting on those who fear Him,
> And His righteousness to children's children,
> To those who keep His covenant
> And remember His precepts to do them. (Psalm 103:17-18)

I was a young wife in ministry, living many miles away from family, so in love, and caring for young children at my feet.

And life was hard.

I was lonely. The church was highly demanding. I seldom saw my husband.

I cried to God and wondered if this is all ministry had to offer. This wasn't what I thought I'd signed up for.

Are you wondering if this is all there is?

God is faithful in every season. Be encouraged. Give every thought, emotion, desire, and disappointment to him.

His loving kindness truly is from everlasting to everlasting.

My Favorite Cake

Recipe from Hilda Pierce, my sweet, amazing cook mother-in-law

1 Duncan Hines Butter Recipe Cake, prepare as directed

Fudge Sauce/Icing:

2 cups white sugar

1/4 cup unsweetened cocoa

2/3 cup milk

1/4 teaspoon salt

2 teaspoons vanilla

1 stick of butter

Begin heating all ingredients but the butter and vanilla, while cake has around ten minutes remaining to bake.

Stir over medium heat and bring to soft boil. Bubble for two minutes. Remove from heat and add butter and vanilla. Stir until butter melts.

While cake is warm, poke holes throughout with a fork. Pour fudge sauce over the cake. Gently pull back small sections of cake and fill with the sauce.

Beat remaining sauce until it thickens and loses its gloss.

Frost a 9 x 13 pan or use eight-inch round pans. If you're using round pans, you should be able to frost the entire cake or allow the icing to drip down the sides.

Chapter 3

The Beautiful Way We Love

Oftentimes, I feel like a mom to the people God has given us.

> Consider it a great joy, my brothers, whenever you experience various trials, knowing that the testing of your faith produces endurance. But endurance must do its complete work, so that you may be mature and complete, lacking nothing. (James 1:2-4)

There is a kind of parental love that comes along with being a pastor's wife. It's difficult to explain the relationship between my church family and me. I love each person in a motherly way, regardless of age.

Most of the time, ministering to and with our family is a joy. We have such a fantastic "seat" at the table.

But then there are seasons of struggles we go through. When there are heartache and heartbreak. "Why's" echo through tear-filled eyes. Hollow eyes betray the strong exterior as fear creeps in. And in my motherly sort of way, I want to fix it. I want to have the perfect words that make it all better, no different from the moment my sweet grandbaby bumps her head and begins to cry.

"Do you want me to kiss it and make it better?"

She walks over and leans in. I kiss her head and hug her. "I'm so sorry you got hurt, baby."

She quits crying and goes back to playing.

The kiss makes it all better.

The trials of this day are far more significant.

As my heart breaks for the people I dearly love, I must resist slipping into:

"If you really loved us, Lord, this would not be happening."

"We serve you Lord, where is the protection that should come our way?"

"You are the Divine Healer … what happened? Did you look the other way?"

And in my search to fix the situation, I am reminded pain or trials in life are never experienced without purpose for those who love God. Among his many promises to his kids, God gives us the only answer to "why?"

James chapter one verses two through four.

Don't get tripped up over the first few words of verse two, those words that tell us to consider it a great joy when we experience these hardships. Don't overlook the next word … KNOWING …

What a gift God gave us in this word. It doesn't say guessing or hoping. KNOWING.

KNOWING what is happening in life produces endurance because as faith is pushed to its limits, we see God keeps his promises. Even better, we can KNOW that it is not endurance just for the sake of enduring. God is right there, active as the endurance becomes complete, so we may be … look at it … look at the last two words of verse four, *LACKING NOTHING.*

I'm no stranger to the personal pain that has caused me to weep, face to the floor, and beg for God's intervention. I have looked toward heaven and wanted him to step in and stop the pain *now*. I confessed that I did not ask for endurance nor did I choose this path toward being complete, lacking nothing.

God, in his great wisdom, loved me deeply as my pain seemed to envelop me. His presence has never been more real than in the aloneness that is found in the dark of night. That time when tears flow freely, and there is no need for the face of "I'm okay."

God has allowed my honesty in weakness. And he is near and is listening as our church family members ache and ask "why?" He is near to you today. Are you asking "why?"

We face the pain of death, cancer, fear, loneliness, addiction, betrayal … what are you facing today?

I wish I could gather you ... each one of you … in my arms and, with motherly love, kiss your forehead and make it all better.

Please remember as you take care of so many people while learning to rely on God yourself, God is for you.

You are in the middle of "complete."

Sing this prayer with me:

> *I need thee every hour ... Most gracious Lord ... No tender voice like thine ... Can peace afford ... I need thee ... oh, I need thee ... Every hour I need thee ... Oh, bless me now my savior ... I come to thee*[3].

Sweet bites of wisdom: "If all struggles and sufferings were eliminated, the spirit would no more reach maturity than would the child." **~Elizabeth Elliott**[4]

Pick up your fork: Read Psalm 66:16-20 and Philippians 3:10-12

Psalm 66:16-20

When we minister to those in our families who have just received devastating news, we know to choose our words carefully. It is not our place to explain why God allows certain things, it is our place to encourage faithfulness because we know he keeps his promises.

I love the Psalms. There's a Psalm for every occasion and emotion.

Read verses 16-20 and record the actions described.

The Psalmist uses these five verses to show us God is faithful to hear, we are to praise him, hatred in our heart would stand between us, and God does not turn his faithful love from us.

How can you use this passage to bring comfort to a friend in time of need?

Philippians 3:10-12

The purpose of every experience in life is to refine us, making us more like Christ. The Apostle Paul and Timothy knew what it meant to give up everything for the cause of Christ. In the previous verses, Paul even compares all he gave up to the filth of garbage.

Whether you are experiencing joys or sorrows, the goal in the midst of it all is spelled out for us in verse ten. What is that goal?

How does keeping the goal in focus help us keep perspective during the challenges life often brings our way?

I love verse twelve. Even Paul admits he is not yet fully mature, but he says he is growing and trying. He gives the reason he reaches for maturity. How can he continue?

How does remembering Christ has taken hold of us push us forward in the face of daily trial?

Chapter 4

Lipstick on His Collar: Graciously Sharing Your Husband While Protecting Your Marriage

The pastor is every woman's spiritual leader, brother, or child.
Learning to share him
and be the gatekeeper at the same time is an art.

> "... But from the beginning of creation, God MADE THEM MALE AND FEMALE. FOR THIS REASON, A MAN SHALL LEAVE HIS FATHER AND MOTHER, AND THE TWO SHALL BECOME ONE FLESH; so they are no longer two, but one flesh. What therefore God has joined together, let no man separate." (Mark 10:6-9)

The year was 1959, and Connie Francis sang a catchy little tune called "Lipstick on Your Collar." The song is a cute, teen-type of love song where she wonders if her date has smooched her best friend.

While the song is lighthearted, the reality of how our enemy slithers around trying to destroy our marriages is serious and heartbreaking. Your husband's downfall would be a prized trophy.

Not long after we married, I noticed my husband's suit lapels often had foundation or blush schmeared on them after church. This was back in the day before preachers wore open-collared or polo shirts.

Before we married, I never paid attention to the amount of "neck hugs" Tommy received after worship. As a young newlywed, makeup on his collar got my attention. I learned my husband was every woman's son or brother. He was loved and appreciated.

Tommy has been very careful over the years to use wisdom when counseling women of any age. Doors are open, or they talk in public areas, and he doesn't counsel for prolonged periods of time. He is happy to help someone dealing with stressful life situations by introducing her to professional Christian counseling services. He even has a rule of never being in a car or eating a meal alone with any woman other than me. These precautions strengthen the trust in each other as well as protect against false accusation or the destructive, sneaky ways of Satan.

I doubt any pastor, who finds himself in a mess of trouble and sin because of an affair, ever set out to do so. The first stopgap to this sin is knowing it could happen to anyone. We are foolish to pretend we are immune to sexual temptation.

Your relationship with Jesus is central to everything you do. As the wife of one who is looked to for advice and sought after by the enemy, you must rely on God to give you the proper perspective as well as discernment. I have experienced on two occasions the need to let my husband know something just didn't "feel right" in my spirit. I'm thankful, instead of telling me I had no reason to be concerned, he listened. While he remained a pastor and spiritual leader in these instances, he was no longer a counselor.

We have been incredibly blessed to experience over twenty-five years in one church. Our children grew up in one home and have a "hometown." We have experienced many moments of laughter as well as sadness through these years, but one thing is sure—when you strive to honor God with your marriage and ministry, he is faithful.

When you have that "not right" feeling, stop and pray. Ask God for his wisdom and discernment. And don't be afraid to talk with your husband about your God-given intuition. We know our husbands are sons, brothers, fathers, and grandfathers to the congregations we call family. God will give us what we need to understand the demand on the pastor's time while protecting the most sacred union on earth.

Perhaps you find yourself this day where you never thought you'd be. Maybe your heart is broken over your husband's choices. I urge you to seek godly counsel and spend time with God unlike you ever have before. We know this heartache is not his will. We also know he loves you and will be faithful in all seasons.

Father, I am happy to be reminded that you created and ordained marriage. I praise you for strong bonds and godly relationships. I ask that you protect your called men and women. I ask for your divine wisdom in ministry. I want to lead and love in a way that honors you and brings others closer to you. I know I cannot do so without your divine guidance and intervention. Please open my eyes and keep me head over heels in love with my husband.

Father, for my sisters in ministry who ache this day, I ask that your Holy Spirit bring comfort, strength, wisdom, and hope. Please protect them from feeling alone and don't allow them to isolate themselves.

Sweet bites of wisdom: "It has been said, and the Bible verifies it, that the greatest need of a man is admiration," she said. "Admire him physically, admire his abilities and admire him spiritually," she advised. Rogers said the goal of her life through all she had been through is "God himself—not peace, nor joy, nor even blessing, but God himself." **—Joyce Rogers**[5]

Pick up your fork: Read 1 Peter 4:1-11

This subject is incredibly personal. Aren't you glad you have a personal Savior?

With verse eleven as your focus, ask yourself, how do speech (both public and private) and actions in your marriage glorify God?

Use this chapter as a springboard for discussion and prayer. If you and your husband have not already established rules that protect your marriage and family, it's time for a date night and conversation that builds a fortress.

I encourage my new friends who are experiencing the pain of broken trust to get godly counsel. You do not have to walk the valley alone.

Chapter 5

Oh No, You Didn't! Drawing the Line in the Sand

Beware of the woman who does not see the pastor as a spiritual leader, brother or child.
Listening to your God-given instincts and handling it correctly.

> Trust in the Lord with all your heart
> and do not lean on your own understanding.
> In all your ways acknowledge Him,
> and He will make your paths straight. (Proverbs 3:5-6)

As the Sunday morning worship service came to a close, my husband stood at the back of the church to shake hands and wish people well. I stood next to him.

And then she walked up.

Walked straight to him.

My husband.

And placed her hand on his chest as she leaned in and said, "Oh, pastor! That message was wonderful!"

I wasn't sure if I should clear my throat loudly or remove her hand or step between them. The other options that ran through my mind aren't fit to print.

She never acknowledged my presence. I wondered if I was a figment of my own imagination.

And my naïve husband didn't seem to notice a problem.

Once we were alone, I let my husband know in no uncertain terms this woman needed to step behind the line. Deep in my gut—I could be spiritual here and use the word spirit, but "gut" is genuinely more fitting—I knew this woman did not view her pastor, *my husband*, as her brother. Needless to say, I stayed close to him when she was around. I introduced myself to her, and there was never another conversation without my interjection.

Ladies, you and I know we cannot stand between our husbands and every woman in the church. It would be a problem in ministry if we allowed jealousy to fill us.

So, what's a wife to do when she sees a female crying on his shoulder or hugging him a little too long? How do we balance protecting the marriage without turning into the green monster?

You might get tired of reading this—but please try not to—you must put your personal relationship with Jesus first in your life. You must choose to grow by reading and studying the Bible and spending time in prayer. Ruth Bell Graham was a beautiful example of how it can be accomplished, even under trying circumstances. "I would go down to my mother's room early in the morning. Her light would be on, and I would find her at her big, flat-top desk," her daughter, Anne Graham Lotz wrote. "She would have about fourteen different translations of the Bible spread out. She would be reading and studying her Bible. I would go down to her room late at night. I would see the light on underneath the door, and I'd go in, and she would be on her knees in prayer."[6]

We serve a God who doesn't play tricks on us. He is the one who told us "Call to me and I will answer (Jeremiah 33:3)."

You and I are imperfect people, and if we rely on instinct alone, we will respond in a less than perfect way.

Trust God with all your heart. Do not trust yourself, or better put—your own understanding. How exactly do you do that?

First, when you find yourself fuming, remove yourself. Walk away. Get by yourself and breathe. Allow time between cause and effect.

Pray and ask God to calm you down and give you wisdom. Ask God to help you know when to speak and when to keep silent.

Once you've allowed some time and have prayed, one of two things will happen. You will either know it is time to talk to your husband, or you will know there is nothing to discuss.

Love your husband with a fierce and protective love. Love him with a gentle and discerning love. Love him with patience and wisdom.

You know, the difficulty that presented itself that Sunday morning resolved through prayer and patience. I'm thankful my husband listened to my heart, and the Lord answered my prayer.

Dear Lord, thank you for a marriage of love and trust. Please help me to rely on you for the wisdom I need to know when to speak and when to wait.

Please watch over your shepherd as he leads. Give him discernment as he ministers.

Help me, as my husband's completer, to remember the vital role you have given me. I want to please you, Lord. I want to have a healthy marriage that honors you.

Sweet bites of wisdom: Train our love ... Discipline it, too ... Deepen it throughout the years, age and mellow it until, time that finds us old without, within, will find us lovers still.
—Ruth Bell Graham, a prayer for her husband, evangelist Billy Graham[7]

Pick Up Your Fork: Read Genesis 2:22-24 and Proverbs 31:10-12

Genesis 2:22-24

After reading the Genesis passage, describe your marriage in three sentences. How does your description compare with God's plan for marriage? What action can you take to strengthen your marriage?

Proverbs 31:10-12

These verses give a beautiful description of a noble wife.

Being the noble wife begins one choice at a time. What actions can you take today that will bring greater trust between you and your husband?

Verse 12 describes the noble wife as one who does good things for her husband all the days of her life. From praying for him every day to listening when he needs a safe place to baking his favorite cake. How will you show your love today?

Chapter 6

Excuse Me, Dear, Didn't You Mean ...: Correcting Your Husband in Public.

There is a time and a place for everything.

> Like apples of gold in settings of silver is a word spoken in right circumstances. (Proverbs 25:11)

My husband and I are a stronger team in ministry than when we first married. Obviously, we know each other better and have learned how to work together. I had been involved in the area of children's ministries even before we married. Fourteen years ago, the church honored me with the responsibility of adding me to the ministerial staff.

Ladies, how many of you want your husband as your boss? I have prayerfully and carefully learned the extra challenges this title brings with it. I've learned from the mistakes I've made. I've especially needed God's guidance with knowing when to speak up. I want my fellow staff members to see me as the overseer of preschool and children's ministries and not the boss's wife.

I don't know the extent in which you are involved in the day to day ministry of the church. Whether you are in meetings or are having a meal with friends, never speak down to or about your husband.

I have been asked if I ever correct my husband or add to his message as he preaches. Oh, my word! No! I have too much respect for the preparation and process of preaching. It's the Holy Spirit's place to add to or change the message. Even should my husband be okay with such an interruption, which would never happen, I cannot imagine my interjection being anything other than a distraction from the most crucial hour of the week.

God's plan for marriage in ministry is teamwork. You are your husband's greatest prayer warrior, cheerleader, sounding board, and safe place. Those moments you hear your husband misquote or say something you know he didn't mean to say, place a reminder in the "we'll talk when we're alone" file. The only disclaimer here is if your husband has asked you to speak up right away.

It isn't popular to say but protecting your husband's ego is a wonderful way to show your love. I hope you're not getting a picture in your mind of a wife looking starry-eyed at her husband, believing he can do no wrong. Simply put, it's a matter of being a support to him instead of undermining his leadership. Whether you are a senior pastor's wife or wife of a pastor on staff, remember how valuable your quiet support is to him.

> *Father, I thank you for the privilege of being the most important person of support to my pastor-husband. I know I can't be the help you intend for me to be without your intervention. I invite you to give me wisdom. I ask that you protect me from myself. Please show me your mercy and grow me closer to you!*

Sweet bites of wisdom: My sweet mother-in-law, a pastor's wife for more than sixty-five years, gave me the advice her pastor's-wife-mom shared with her before she married. "Hilda, remember—you are not the pastor. Your husband is. Pray for him every day. Be there for him when he needs you." **—Hilda Pierce[8]**

Pick Up Your Fork: Read Proverbs 15:4 and James 3:5-12

Proverbs 15:4

I love how the scripture paints a vivid picture! Proverbs 15:4 describes the power of words. Print three "I can" statements of specific ways your words can be a tree of life for your husband.

Perversion in our speech will crush the spirit. What an excellent description of what happens to the men in our lives when we speak to them in a way that tears down. Spend time in prayer and ask God to show you ways you degrade your husband unknowingly by the words you speak. What will you do to change your pattern and be a tree if life?

James 3:5-12

We usually consider James 3 in the context of how we speak in general to and about others. Reread this passage, applying it directly to your speech pattern towards your husband. I believe there are ways you are already very successful as you relate these verses personally.

As uncomfortable as you might be, where do you see yourself in light of this passage? What changes are you challenged to make?

How will you choose to use the power of your words from this day forward?

Chapter 7

He is Not Yours Alone: Your Husband's Absence on Christmas Day

Death doesn't take a vacation. Sometimes you need to be creative with your family time.

> But the fruit of the Spirit is love, joy, peace, patience, kindness, goodness, faithfulness, gentleness, self-control; against such things there is no law. (Galatians 5:22-23)

The morning was cozy-perfect. The Christmas tree stood in the corner of the family room. A cheery fire crackling in the fireplace, happy sounds of children playing with their just opened gifts, and the wonderful aromas already coming from the still in progress Christmas meal.

My husband and I have enjoyed cooking together for many years, especially for holiday meals! Good times in the Pierce home!

Until the phone rang.

The young man at the other end of the line tried to be strong as he spoke. He was sorry for bothering us on Christmas day, but his dad was not expected to live much longer. Could Pastor Tommy please come?

It was easy just to give Tommy a kiss and ask that he deliver the message we were praying.

The kids weren't happy about their dad leaving that morning. Honestly, I felt a twinge of "Can't someone else go?" Once he was on his way, I had a choice to make. I could sulk and be upset along with the kids, or I could help them understand what it means to be a pastor.

What a privilege to be near a family during their most difficult days. The role of the pastor is one of caregiver, shepherd, and friend. When he is called to a grieving family, your husband needs your understanding and support.

The next time his cell phone rings and he must go, take this opportunity to have a conversation with the kids that will help them feel grateful for what Dad is doing rather than resentful. Age-appropriate questions are great discussion starters.

What does Daddy do for a living? This question gives you the opportunity to talk about what goes on when he is not preaching. You might be surprised to find your kids think that's all he does. Help them make a list of all the things Dad does Monday through Sunday. The family might have fun going over the list with him when he gets home.

Why do you think people want to talk with Daddy when they are sad, afraid, or sick? Here's where you can help your children understand what being a shepherd means. Just as Jesus is the Good Shepherd, the pastor is the shepherd of the church. He is an example of God's love as he listens to, reads scripture and prays with, and helps people to remember God is faithful.

What can we do while we wait for Daddy to get home? Your kids will love this one because the answers will help them understand they are a part of God's family. Here's your opportunity to teach the power of prayer. Stop what you are doing and pray together for Dad and the people he is helping. This is also a time for kids to be honest about how they feel about Dad's absence. Our kids need to know it's okay to be upset if we use the feelings we have to learn more about God's promise to use everything for good in our lives.

Your support during the tough calls away from home makes it possible for your husband to take care of people in a way that honors God.

Tommy was gone several hours that Christmas day. The young man's dad died not long after my husband arrived. He was able to be the pastor and shepherd they needed. The kids learned the importance of the pastor in the lives of the church family, especially when faced with the death of a loved one.

Instead of holding on to the twinge of "let someone else do it," I asked God to give me compassion for the family who called. I was humbled to learn they said goodbye to a wonderful husband and dad that day, while people all over the world were in celebration mode.

Tommy's absence that morning was not a sacrifice for us, but rather a privilege.

> *Hello God, it's me again. Sometimes I get so tired of being the one who has to understand, the one who must help the kids understand. I need you, Lord. Please help me to be patient and understanding. Instead of thinking of myself, help me to remember to pray for my husband as he deals with difficulties in the lives of the people we serve.*
>
> *I can't do this on my own. I need you to give me a heart that is compassionate for the hurting. Help me to be creative in teaching my children what it means to be a shepherd.*
>
> *Thank you, Lord, for your example of love and for giving us the tools we need to please you. I love you, Lord.*

Sweet bites of wisdom: I think I was disappointed with myself. I had to come to terms with the fact that I wasn't the "good little missionary wife" I always thought I was or wanted to be. And the strain of being both mom and dad to three small children under school age, as well as my mission responsibilities, just got to me in the end. I started complaining to God thinking that no one else would know. But of course, that stuff shows. Stuart noticed what I tried to pretend wasn't bothering me. He said, "Jill, I can't do this work unless you're with me in it."

I shared this struggle with my senior missionary, and she was the friend who helped me to realize that if this was what God wanted for this period of our lives, I would not be happy if my husband were home. Once I got that sorted out in my head, it filtered down to my heart. I saw that it was the will of God that Stuart go, and I accepted that, expecting that it would be for a lifetime. **—Jill Briscoe**[9]

Pick up your fork: Read Matthew 22:34-40

I love to study and teach from the Gospels. Sometimes what I read makes me super uncomfortable. Today's short passage makes me nervous when I slow down and really take it in.

The Sadducees and Pharisees were always trying to trick Jesus with their questions. In the previous verses, we read Jesus' response to the Sadducees.

He basically shut them down. Verse 34 describes it like this: "He silenced them." I love that!

The Pharisees took their own shot. An expert with the law asked Jesus a test question. "Which commandment in the law is the greatest?"

Jesus' response is something that challenges me every time I read or teach it. Love God with all my heart, soul, and mind … and love my neighbor as myself. I try to imagine what this love looks like. To love God with all my heart, soul, and mind is a love that is all in. Fully committed. Trusting him with everything. It's a love that takes action.

What does it look like in you? First, as a mom. What do the kids see in you that makes them know you love God?

As a pastor's wife, how does this love for God present itself when your husband is called away right before the birthday candles have been lit?

Now that pesky little verse 39—love your neighbor as yourself. Your neighbor is at the other end of that phone call.

Here's where it gets uncomfortable, knowing Jesus said to love my neighbor as myself. Read through this short passage again and apply it fully to the moment the phone rings. How will this kind of love change your perspective?

Write a prayer that begins with confession, moves to request for the right response, and concludes with praise for God's love and provision.

Lemon Supreme Special Cake

1 Lemon Supreme cake mix

1 cup apricot nectar

3/4 cup oil

4 eggs

1/2 cup white sugar

Blend cake mix, sugar, oil, and apricot nectar until combined.

Add eggs, one at a time.

Bake in a prepared tube pan at 325° for 1 hour.

Cool upright in pan for 15 minutes.

Place cake on serving plate.

Icing

Mix 1 cup confectioners' sugar and the juice of one lemon. Glaze cake while it is still warm.

Chapter 8

Your Kids Are Like Eli's Sons: Protecting and Teaching Your Children Under Attack

Biblical guidance for your children when they are guilty, and when they are falsely accused.

> So you shall observe to do just as the Lord your God has commanded you; you shall not turn aside to the right or to the left. (Deuteronomy 5:32)

They were in the conference room. Seemed as if they had been there for an eternity. It was a meeting called by parents of a girl who accused our older daughter of saying hurtful things about her. I wasn't allowed in the meeting. I prayed for truth to be known and for protection for my family.

Our son and another boy played basketball together one afternoon. I watched them play. Our son took a shot, and the ball came down on the other boy's head. Our son ran over and asked if he was okay. He apologized, and they continued to play. A few days later, I found myself in my husband's office. We were seated with the boy and his parents. His parents were demanding another apology.

From the moment our kids are born, they are placed in a different category from all other kids. They are assigned the unfair title of perfection. No pastor's family likes it. The kids didn't ask for it. Some church families are easier on the kids than others. Sadly, it's just a fact in ministry.

My husband and I have four children. You can imagine, we've been in the "hot seat" many times over the years. Our parenting wasn't perfect, nor were our kids. My husband has served in only four churches during our marriage. The last twenty-eight plus years have been in the fourth church.

This means our children know one church home. That is highly unusual for today's pastor's families. Over the years we have been super blessed by people who love our kids unconditionally and super challenged by those who place unfair expectations on them.

Our children are all adults now. They are wonderful people, and we are proud of them. You can guess, though, when they were growing up, they made their fair share of mistakes. We made our fair share of parenting woes as well.

Whether guilty or not, nothing cuts deeper than watching your children hurt. We cannot control the ways and times our kids mess up, nor can we control the response of the people in our church families.

You and your husband must be the same people on Monday morning that you claim to be on Sundays. Blameless in that you are people of integrity. You practice what you preach. You are for real. In other words, your children could wholeheartedly speak for you and say you are the real deal.

What are the biblical guidelines for teaching and disciplining our kids?

Look back at Deuteronomy 5:32. Observe to do just as the Lord has commanded you. His commandments for parenting are the same no matter who you are. Teach the children of God's saving grace. Teach the children to love God. Teach the children his statutes, his precepts. In other words, teach the children the Bible.

Love one another. Be forgiving. Practice the fruit of the spirit. Trust in God and not yourself.

So back to the beginning of this chapter. How do you, hands-on, deal with accusations?

First, address the elephant in the room. You might have to address it many times. Acknowledge the fact your kids already know—people call them out for things no other kids get called on. The expectations are high.

Remind your kids God's expectations for them are the same as his expectations for you and for every believer. God wants us to love him with all our heart and bring him honor with our lives.

If your child is guilty of wrongdoing, the first step is getting it right with God. That's church-ese for asking forgiveness. The second step is getting it right with people. Again, seeking forgiveness from whoever was offended. That's a tough one because we need to teach our children that not all people are willing to forgive.

The type of discipline varies as many ways as there are personalities. You know your child and what is effective, growth producing discipline.

If your child is falsely accused, the first step is allowing the child to voice how this makes her feel. Agree with her that it stinks. Read together the story of Joseph. This is a biblical example of one who was falsely accused yet he chose to do the right thing. God took care of Joseph.

What is the right thing? Love, forgive, and remain faithful to God.

Everything worked out between my daughter and the family she and her dad met with that morning. We are friends to this day. Unfortunately, not all stories have happy endings. The folks we met with in my husband's office about our son left the church.

Dear God, parenting in this glass house is hard. I often times don't even know what to do. Please protect our kids from false accusations. Give my husband and me wisdom to see through lies, whether told by our kids or by someone accusing them.

Place deep in the hearts of our children a love for you and a desire to be obedient. Help us know how to teach our children to honor you.

Thank you for this incredible privilege of raising children to know you!

Sweet bites of wisdom: People sometimes look at my family and think there's something picture-perfect about us. I know this because people tell me. And though I would never want to minimize the profound blessing of beautiful children and a husband who is a godly, great guy, the truth is that *my family is not perfect, and neither is yours.* Up close, you'll see all the ways that our fur is less than sparkling white. And up close, I'll see all those things about you, too. **—Elisha Galotti**[10]

Pick up your fork: Read Proverbs 22:6 and Deuteronomy 6:1-9

Proverbs 22:6

This verse challenges us as parents to teach each of our children in the ways he or she learns best. The same biblical truths taught in different ways. Take a moment and write down a description of your children, each personality and the specific ways they learn. In each instance, how can you teach God's truths "in the way" he or she should go? In other words, in the way he or she learns best.

Deuteronomy 6:1-9

These verses refer to the Ten Commandments given in the previous chapter. We teach these rules for life to our children, not only to hold them to the standard of keeping them, but so they will recognize their need for a savior. They were given to be obeyed. The only way any of us can abide by them is with God's help.

How can you model and teach these rules for living in everyday, practical ways? Look for life application opportunities. Be ready to talk about the reasons God gave us these rules for living.

Chapter 9

Ministry Isn't for Sissies: Weathering the Storms

What should you do when you don't know what to do?

> Now may the God of hope fill you with all joy and peace in believing, so that you will abound in hope by the power of the Holy Spirit. (Romans 15:13)

Many years ago, when our third child was just an infant, we faced a situation that came from inside the church. A leader in the church met my husband at the door after worship one Sunday. As he shook Tommy's hand and smiled, he let my husband know it was time to start preaching sermons that made people feel good. This simple statement was the beginning of the end of our service with this particular church home. In the following months, we experienced everything from face-to-face threats to prank phone calls. One threat was to expect to find ourselves homeless and jobless.

You can imagine my panic as I held my newborn and watched two children under the age of four as they played.

What will happen to us, Lord?

Why are you allowing this, Lord?

Haven't we been faithful, Lord?

I had no friend I could call. We lived many miles from my family. This was pre-cell phone days, so long distant phone calls were costly. Tommy went to work each morning, facing the difficulties of the day at the office. I was home with the children, often afraid to answer the phone for fear of what I might hear.

The battle was real.

This was spiritual warfare.

The first of many heartbreaking battles to come over the space of years together.

Fear tried to steal every ounce of joy I had. Instead of acting on faith, believing that God had everything under control, I cried out in panic. It was a helpless feeling to watch my husband in defeat, weary, and bruised.

We have choices to make when faced with the unknown. During these kinds of difficulties, we have to decide if we really believe all the things we have taught about a mighty, loving God. To put it another way, this is where the rubber hits the road.

What do you do when you don't know what to do? You do what you know to do.

What do I know to do? In everything, give thanks and make my requests known to God. Pray.

I'm not talking about an add-on to the blessing at mealtime or an addendum following now I lay me down to sleep. This is the kind of prayer following the pattern of King David. He poured his heart out to God in 100 percent honesty.

No matter what else I said between Dear God and Amen, the cry of my heart was "help me trust you fully."

What do I know to do? Open my Bible and read the numerous and familiar passages that remind me God is sovereign, God is mighty, and God has a plan for my family.

What do I know to do? Say it out loud! Speak faith to my children and my husband. Not just words, but faith words. Believe in my heart that God will take care of our family no matter what and say it out loud.

What do I know to do? Praise him! God lives in the praise of his people. When we sing and say words of praise, the enemy runs away. Praise him for the obvious—the air we breathe, the warmth of the sun, and the ability to think. Search our lives for the less obvious and praise him for the dirty dishes in the sink, the neighbor's dog that barks at all hours, and junk mail.

No matter the circumstance, these are the things we know to do. Not just one, but all. Pray, read, speak, and praise.

When the storm clouds cleared, we found that God used those terrible days and nights to bring us to a new church home. Our little family went from a place where we felt like the hired hands to a place that made us family.

Father, sometimes I can't see beyond my pain and fear to be able to trust you. I need your presence not only in my heart but next to me wherever I am. I need to feel your peace.

Please protect my family from an attack that destroys. Bring us closer together and closer to you. Please protect my heart from growing bitter with disappointment.

And Father? No matter what happens next, please give my husband and me the faith we need to stand firm on your promises.

I praise you for this calling. I praise you for my home and my family. I praise you for giving my husband a purpose on this earth, a mission that brings people into a relationship with you. I praise you for who you are. I love you, Lord!

Sweet bites of wisdom: There are ministry wives who are like a wounded soldier with scars, wounds, even some fresh bandages. Been there? Scary right? Post-Traumatic Stress Disorder (PTSD) is a debilitating condition among Pastor's Wives. Their handicap leaves them to suffer alone. As someone goes to hug them, they unintentionally rip a scab off an old wound … leaving it bleeding and hurting all over again. She then is tormented by flashbacks of the hurt for days or weeks. It's best for everyone if she stays at a distance. She accepts her life as a martyr, or she eventually gives up altogether. This is a reality. Another reality is that healing is possible through the power of Christ. Psalms 46:1 is clear who can save us from this prison of desolation … *"God is our refuge and strength, a very present help in trouble."* God is "very present" … our husband, best friend, mom, etc. can't always be there. The Great Comforter is there. He created the universe, but he also wants to be the creator of refuge and strength for us! **—Shonda Kuehl**[11]

Pick up your fork: Read Ephesians 3:14-20

Notice verse 14 "for this reason." For what reason? The passage prior reminds us in Jesus we have boldness, access to him, and confidence to be able to face afflictions and hardships. Paul wants us to be firmly planted in the love of God.

Read verses 14-16. What does it mean to you to be granted power through the Holy Spirit? How does it change your perspective?

Verses 17-19. What must you do to be filled with the fullness of God?

Verses 20-21. Will you stop and give God all the glory for what he is doing in your life? In your husband's life? Even in the most painful moments, will you choose to give God glory because you can trust him?

Chapter 10

The Struggle is Real: Supporting Him on Mondays

Many of the most powerfully used pastors throughout history suffered from depression. Praying your husband through the down days.

> The LORD also will be a stronghold for the oppressed,
> A stronghold in times of trouble;
> And those who know Your name will put their trust in You,
> For You, O LORD, have not forsaken those who seek You. (Psalm 9:9-10)

In 2011, Thom S. Rainer wrote an article titled "When Pastors Experience Depression."[12] He discussed several probable causes for depression, such as spiritual warfare, unrealistic expectations, and greater platforms for critics. I was intrigued by the comments that followed the article. Many pastors thanked him for his candid look at the issue and the suggestions for help. Several mentioned the urge to quit on Mondays. A few talked about the dreaded blinking message light at the office on Mondays, knowing most of the time an angry, offended voice was on the other end. Tommy has often stated even one hundred *attaboys* cannot quiet the one discontented voice.

A quick look through history shows us depression in ministry, while growing, is not new. Charles Spurgeon, known as the Prince of Preachers, was known to suffer great bouts of depression. He said he could weep for hours like a child and yet not understand why he was crying.[13]

The great Martin Luther knew the battle with depression. The episodes were "always marked by the same features: a feeling of profound aloneness, a sense that God was singling him out for suffering, a loss of faith that God is good and good to me, and a resulting inward self-reliance."[14]

Jonathan Edwards, often referred to as America's Greatest Theologian, suffered spells of exhaustion, depression, and illness. He is known for his sermon "Sinners in the Hands of an Angry God."[15]

David struggled with depression. He certainly had good cause. King Saul hunted him like a dog. Saul was out for blood and why? David had done nothing but obey and honor God. Scriptures give us a glimpse into David's dark hours.

Pastors who lead churches in multiple services each Sunday, and pastors who preach to a congregation of twenty, understand the oppression of depression. While depression has many sources, I believe spiritual warfare is at its core.

I wish this chapter could be a live conversation. Many of you would freely talk about your husband's discouragement on Monday morning, or possibly even as soon as Sunday at lunch. I wish I had a quarter for every lunch conversation that began with "I didn't see so and so today" or "So and so hasn't been in worship in x number of weeks."

I used to urge him to focus on the full seats. On Monday mornings, after he listened to the blinking light, I'd try to tell him God is not finished with him yet. I would try to fix it all and make everything better.

But you know what? I cannot do that. In fact, it isn't even my place. And you cannot do it either.

My place—and your place—is to listen, and more importantly, to pray.

Innate in our nurturing nature is to kiss it and make it all better. Maybe, you are like me, and are a cheerleader! When he stands in front of you, ready to quit, your first response is to jump up with a "Ready! Okay!" You interrupt him and tell him he is wrong. It's going to be okay. You tell him to stop thinking that way. And soon enough, he stops coming to you with his empty heart.

You realize, this means he isn't talking to anyone if he isn't communicating with you.

So be quiet.

Listen.

And pray.

Pray for yourself as his confidant. Knowing you cannot fix it is the first step to being the best help to him. Give your husband, the ministry, the feelings, the despair—give it all to God. Give your desire to fix him to God. Submit to the Holy Spirit and be still.

Pray for your husband. Ask God to protect him and teach him, to be near to him and bring him peace. Ask God to send people to speak positive words to him. Ask God to use these times to make your sweet husband more Christ-like.

At the end of each day and the dawn of each morning, you must trust God to be who he says he is. Trust God to be the one to accomplish his purpose.

Sit.

Listen.

Love.

To the One who created and knows my husband, my heart is heavy. Sometimes I feel so angry and sometimes sad but always helpless. Remind me of your love for your church and your preacher. Remind me of your sovereignty and control. Help me to trust you with the one I love most on earth.

Forgive me for trying to fix things on my own. Please forgive me for being self-sufficient.

Help me to be still and listen. Help me to weigh my words carefully.

Please use the down times to make us more like you.

I give you all honor and praise for working in ways I cannot see.

I trust you, Lord. I love you.

Sweet bites of wisdom: Be available. He needs your love, your words of affirmation, and most of all your unconditional support. Be there when he needs to talk, when he needs some TLC and even when he needs just to veg out and do nothing! He wants to know that you will follow his lead, no matter what. Not easy as a wife, but absolutely essential. We are in a fight for our marriages and husbands, and our husbands are worth fighting for! God's name and glory are worth it! **—Heather Platt**[16]

Pick up your fork: Read Psalm 40:1-3 and 1 Peter 5:6-7

I wish you could tell me—how you doin'? As you read about your husband's depression struggles, did your heart shout "What about me?" You're not alone.

Psalm 40:1-3

These verses are for you today.

Verse one: The Psalmist waited patiently for the Lord. Who or what do you turn to and expect relief from your sadness?

What is your first response when you read the rest of verse one?

Verses two and three describe the power of God to reach us where we are and meet our deepest need. What is your most profound need today?

God knows your husband's most profound need as well. Will you stop at this moment, and release him to God's care?

1 Peter 5:6-7

Verse six: What beautiful instructions for his kids! Choose four words to describe the feelings this verse brings to the surface.

What does it mean to cast?

What does it mean to cast your cares upon him?

Close your eyes and think in pictures. See yourself handing those cares to God. List those cares here.

Wolves Among Us: Self-Control and Bites of Sweet Freedom

> Now for this very reason also, applying all diligence, in your faith supply moral excellence, and in your moral excellence, knowledge, and in your knowledge, self-control, and in your self-control, perseverance, and in your perseverance, godliness, and in your godliness, brotherly kindness, and in your brotherly kindness, love. (1 Peter 1:5-7)

I've heard this quote from many sources, and you have as well. My husband has repeated this one saying many times to our kids over the years. Even as he says the words, he recognizes they are easy to say and challenging to do.

"You cannot control what people say or do, but you can control how you respond."

Shew!

That advice is easy to give, but when someone has mistreated you—or worse yet, your family—it's another story. You want to shout "It's on!" Well, okay, maybe you don't want to yell it but true confession, sometimes I do. Of course, I remain self-controlled because I would never knowingly bring shame to my husband or the church.

I ask myself if my response would be different if I were not a pastor's wife. What if I didn't wear that title? The Holy Spirit reminds me, the title that makes a difference in me is not that of Mrs., but the title Child of God. I never choose knowingly to bring shame to the name of Jesus.

That said, how do you respond to the wolves among us?

Connie Faulkner Pie

By Connie Faulkner

1/2 stick melted butter

1-1/2 cups white sugar

3 tablespoons of unsweetened cocoa

1 teaspoon vanilla

1/2 cup evaporated milk

2 eggs

1 unbaked pie shell

Mix all ingredients together at medium speed for one minute or until smooth. Pour into pie shell and bake for 10 minutes at 400° degrees. Reduce heat to 350° and bake 25 minutes longer.

Serve with whipped topping or ice cream.

You might want to go ahead and bake two. It'll become a family favorite at first bite.

Chapter 11

If I Had Known Then: Well, You Couldn't Have Known Then, So Stop That

The biblical response to regrets and the future.

> Brethren, I do not regard myself as having laid hold of it yet; but one thing I do: forgetting what lies behind and reaching forward to what lies ahead, I press on toward the goal for the prize of the upward call of God in Christ Jesus. (Philippians 3:13-14)

I turned eighteen in September and married my best friend in November. I knew we would see lives changed, have tons of fun in countless Vacation Bible Schools, and get the privilege of bringing our own kids up in the church. I expected friendships that would last a lifetime and pie in the sky when we die by and by.

It honestly never occurred to me that some would use my friendship to gain the senior pastor's ear, or worse yet, there would be people within the church who would actively choose to harm our family's reputation.

I admit I've spent too much time going over past difficulties and imagining better outcomes. If I had known then … I could have.

What a colossal waste of time and energy.

The apostle Paul tells us to put the past in perspective. Leave it behind us. We have a hard time with that, don't we?

If we have been hurt in the past, we have a way of expecting new folks to hurt us in the same way. Without thinking, we don't give God a chance to bring us friendship and good and perfect things through his people, because we have already stamped them as "predator."

We give Satan the keys to our thoughts. We allow him to remind us of past failures. We let him steal a happy day by shoving us back into the memories of who said and did what. We even revel in it.

How unfair to people and tragic in the face of God!

Regrets can destroy a person. It doesn't matter if the disappointments are caused by you or done to you, the past cannot change. The only thing the negative experiences of the past can do is eat away at your future.

Have a plan in place for those moments when regrets and bad memories raise their heads. Choose favorite Bible verses and passages to read at a moment's glance. Respond to the temptation to "go there" by praying. God will get you through it if you rely on him.

Paul also said to press forward and reach for the high calling. God has a plan for you. The calling in ministry is full of opportunity. You and I have a choice to make every morning. We either choose God's grace, forgiveness, and grand design or we remain paralyzed in the mud of what was.

Have I oversimplified it? I don't think so. I'm there with you, every day. I know the feeling of turning the corner in the grocery store and bumping smack into someone who was once a good friend. The flood of emotion, the memories of laughter that are lost to the fresher memory of betrayal. It has wrecked many a good day for me. Too many.

I'm making my own choice to trust God for the new day instead of allowing bitterness to grow out of what I can't change.

The prize is in our future. I believe the prize begins with obedience and it will finish when we see Jesus.

I don't want to have to hang my head because I brought shame to his name with my choices. My goal? To bring him honor today.

To the One Who Knows and Understands, I give the past to you. Please forgive me for the days I did not honor you. I want to live to honor you with what I say and do. Protect me from myself and my selfish ways.

I need your help to forgive those who hurt me. I can't put it behind me without your Holy Spirit. Please remove the thoughts that take me back to the painful days.

I praise you for providing for me. Thank you for the goodness of a new day. Thank you for the gift of salvation.

Thank you for the ability to choose you.

Sweet bites of wisdom: Control the controllables, leave the uncontrollables to God.
—Kay Warren[17]

Pick up your fork: Read 1 Peter 5:6-7 and Deuteronomy 8

1 Peter 5:6-7

What does it mean to humble yourself before the Lord? The late great Reverend Billy Graham often spoke of humbling ourselves. He said first and foremost, confess your sins and ask forgiveness. He also advised we need to be patient when going through false accusations of hurtful experiences.

Have you humbled yourself today through the confessing of your sin?

Are you carrying age-old burdens? Yesterday's troubles? God says cast them on over, you don't need them. He can handle it. Write a prayer, describe the burdens you carry and why they are painful. Give them to God.

Deuteronomy 8

Choosing an Old Testament passage to apply to the future might seem odd. Read the chapter and take note each time we are instructed to keep God's commandments. Obedience is key.

Look at verses 11-14. When God brings success, what does he caution? What are we to remember?

Locate the verse that tells why God gives success in any area of life.

Chapter 12

Wolves in Sheep's Clothing: Those Who Seek to Hurt

David turned to God for protection and wisdom. You can too.

> Be on guard for yourselves and for all the flock, among which the Holy Spirit has made you overseers, to shepherd the church of God which He purchased with His own blood. (Acts 20:28-29)

"Momma, are we moving?" My young son looked up at me with large, questioning blue eyes.

"No, why would you ask?"

"Because I heard that lady over there say 'Don't worry, Tommy will be gone soon enough.' I thought that meant we're moving."

"I'm sure you misunderstood. Don't worry. This is our church home."

When I saw who my son heard talking, I knew it was not a good thing. This wolf had lurked for several years. Her one goal in life seemed to be to make ministry for Tommy miserable enough to walk away.

I hate to put it in writing, but it's a reality. We have dealt with heartbreaking rumors in the community and straight up lies within the church. The most painful experiences came from people we thought were our friends.

I don't know any minister who enjoys this subject. It's painful. It's discouraging. It can lead to a faith crisis. It can take years to heal.

So, how do we function in ministry? How do we love people and work together to spread the gospel, when we aren't sure who we can trust?

Troublemakers are nothing new. Recognizing it is reality is the first step. But may I please caution you, don't allow yourself to become paranoid. Don't slip into thinking everyone is out to get you.

God has given us words of wisdom to live by. Be on guard. Trust in him and not our own understanding. Love each other. Forgive each other.

God reminds us in many passages, he is willing to help us when we rely on him. His Holy Spirit has a way of telling us when to speak and when to be quiet. We don't even need to understand the why's of the message of "hush," we just need to obey.

I stood talking with several ladies one Sunday morning. As we rambled from one subject to the next, I thought of a humorous story to tell. As soon as the thought crossed my mind, I knew I was to keep quiet. The message was loud and clear—don't tell the story. I reasoned with myself. The story was harmless, yet funny. So, in all my lack of wisdom, I told it. The ladies laughed, and we went on our way.

I felt my disobedience immediately. I felt sick over it the rest of the day. That evening, I prayed and asked God to forgive me. I also knew I owed the ladies an apology. I knew I wouldn't see them again for at least a week, so I wrote out my apologies. I explained I knew as I told the story I was to keep my mouth shut. I asked for their forgiveness.

When I saw them again, I was amazed that none of them remembered what I was referring to. Not one. I'm glad God loves me enough to discipline me. I am pretty sure it was a practice lesson. Since only God knows who is waiting for me to fail, and who is a true friend, I've learned to trust his prompting. When he says, "Zip it!" my mouth is zipped!

One of my favorite passages is Matthew 5-7, known as the Sermon on the Mount. Jesus taught a lengthy lesson on living to please and honor God. He describes the one who hears his words and acts on them like the man who built his house on the rock. Take time to study these chapters, the words will help you grow wise.

Can you prevent an attack from a wolf that looks like a sheep? Nope. Can you be strong enough in your relationship with Jesus to turn to him for what you need to get through it? Yup.

It would be a wonderful thing if I could tell you it's going to get better. It isn't gonna get better, but I can promise you it will be okay. Ministry is frontline spiritual warfare stuff. The best news is, we can read the final chapter. We know how all this ends. Remain faithful.

By the way, it was difficult for a season as the lady tried to rid the church family of the Pierces. Through prayer, perseverance, and the support of real sheep, God provided for every need!

To the Giver of every perfect thing, I praise you for your faithfulness!

I admit, knowing there may be people in our church family who are out to cause trouble is more than unsettling.

Please protect your church. Please protect my family. Please protect your servant.

I know I need to trust you and remember nothing takes you by surprise. I also need help remembering you love all people. Help me to love them too.

Help me to be wise as a serpent and as gentle as a dove. I want to honor you with my words and actions.

Lord, be glorified!

Sweet bites of wisdom: There is the issue to friendships within the church or ministry; the common struggle of loneliness felt by many and for some, the desire to shun the spotlight even though your husband is in it all of the time. These concerns must be dealt with and not buried to prevent what we have sadly seen in too many cases. How many ministries have been damaged or even destroyed because the ministry wife was so unhappy, discontent or bitter that her husband was forced to resign? Please don't let that happen to you. Satan would love nothing better than to use issues like these to drive a wedge through your marriage and then your ministry. Be on alert for warning signs. Stay connected to the Lord through prayer and the consistent study of his Word. Seek godly counsel through a mentor. Praise God for the results. ~ **Mary Mohler**[18]

Pick Up Your Fork: Read 2 Thessalonians 2:13-17 and 2 Timothy 4:1-5

2 Thessalonians 2:13-17

Paul expressed thanks for the people of Thessalonica as he reminded them of their calling to believe in the truth. Verse 15 begins with the words "So then" or "Therefore."

What does it mean to stand firm? Think about a challenging experience in your life. Did you stand firm? How did it help you to push through?

List the ways God gives encouragement and hope during the trying days in ministry.

What are the good works and deeds God uses to strengthen you?

2 Timothy 4:1-5

Paul charged Timothy with responsibilities that also belong to today's Christians.

Paul was no stranger to persecution and danger. He understood the weight of his words and yet he gave clear instructions. What reasons did he give for the urgency at hand?

Verse five is one to commit to memory. When the going gets tough and the enemy attacks, this verse is a shield as well as marching orders for our next move. How does it encourage you to remain faithful? What ministry are you charged to fulfill?

Chapter 13

Please Pray for Me: Praying for Others While Your Own Heart is Breaking

Your strength to help others during your own time of need comes from God. Practical tips for tapping into God's power in your life.

> The Lord is my strength and my shield;
> My heart trusts in Him, and I am helped;
> Therefore my heart exults,
> And with my song I shall thank Him. (Psalm 28:7)

My mother was in the final stages of lung cancer. Her time on earth was coming to an end. I was saying goodbye to someone so dear to me I couldn't imagine life without her. I spent a few weeks with her and had to return home. I didn't want to leave her. We cried together and hugged the kind of hug where neither wanted to be the first to let go.

And I journeyed home.

Soon after, my heart bleeding out inside me, I found myself listening to the needs of some of my church family. I'll admit, part of me wanted to hold my hand up and announce "Stop! Not today. I can't. I just can't." Even as I listened, I wondered "Can he not see my eyes are empty? Does she not see I am barely half committed to this conversation?"

I heard myself say, "Yes, I'll pray for you" and "I'm so sorry you are going through this." I wanted to say, "Please, please pray for my momma. Please pray for me to be able to trust God in these coming days. Please. Pray for me."

Those I listened to that day were aware of my mom's need for prayer. They knew my heart ached. And yet, they did not ask how I was doing. They were too wrapped up in their own need.

I went home that day feeling drained and empty. I found myself wallowing in self-pity.

And God's gentle voice whispered a reminder. I wasn't designed to bear sorrow's burden alone. And even though it is a beautiful thing when God's people come around, my first place for relief should never be other people. It shouldn't even be my husband.

The LORD is my strength and my shield. When my heart trusts in him, I am helped.

When I think back on that day, I realize I had done very little to keep that kind of experience from happening. I don't mean I should have hidden in the choir robe room or worn a disguise to church. I had not spent time with the Lord that morning. I didn't bother to talk with him about my pain. I methodically got dressed and drove to church.

In other words, I walked in unarmed. I set myself up for hurt feelings on top of a bleeding heart.

God has gifted us first ladies in many ways. One gift that it seems we have in common is the ability to listen to and pray for others. It doesn't always feel like a gift. Especially when we are wrapped up in our own concern for our kids, the health of someone we love, or big decisions that need to be made.

But, gifted we are!

God wants all believers, not just the preacher's wife, to sit with him first thing and bring our heartache to him. He is waiting to be our strength and shield. He is waiting to be our help. So let's set the example and show our church family the difference God makes when we rely on him.

First, spend time in prayer and reading some of the many scriptures that feed the soul. Ask God to fill us up, so we can be a blessing in the lives around us. When the Holy Spirit brings his comfort and strength to our need, we are able to listen to the needs of others and really hear them.

Second, trust God to use our heartache for our good and for the good of those he sends our way. He promised to bring good through all things for those who love him. Don't allow your pain to be wasted. Know that if you are grasping for help for an addicted child, struggling with food issues, holding on to an injury from childhood, or wishing your husband would treat you like he did when you first married, so are the people around you.

And finally, when you get in your car, ask God to give you a heart of compassion for those who hurt. Ask him to protect you from comparing their need to your own need. Trust him to be faithful.

You know, those folks that poured their hearts out to me that morning did not have my pain on their radar. I doubt it will ever dawn on them, perhaps I needed an ear as badly as they did. But it's okay. Because I learned a valuable lesson that day. I learned when God said to come to him, he meant it. When I go to him, he gently moves my pain aside and replaces it with his peace.

Don't leave your house empty and expect your church family to fill you up. The LORD is waiting.

> *To the One who knows me best and loves me most, help me to rely on your strength. I admit I have times of wishing it could be about me for a change and not about the next church member who needs a shoulder to cry on. I want to sit with you and allow your strength to fill me to overflowing.*
>
> *Please give me a heart of compassion. Help me to point the people you have sent my way to you for all they need.*
>
> *Thank you for being faithful to your word. Thank you for using everything in my life for your glory and my good. And thank you for the people in my life, my church family, given to me to love. Help me to point them to you.*

Sweet bites of wisdom: I know when my life gets out of *whack*, there is always one common denominator: a neglected prayer life. When we ignore that time alone with the Lord, our resources (patience, long-suffering, love, hope, etc.) are exhausted—used up. We begin to run on fumes. After a while, an emotional and spiritual crash happens and manifest itself as depression. Sometimes, we shop to try to "fix" things a bit. Other times, we try to lose weight. It doesn't fill the void either. The vacuum is too big and is often our own doing. We moved from the Lord. He didn't. We did. **—Teri Brooks**[19]

Pick up your fork: Read 2 Corinthians 1:3-4 and Psalm 119:49-50

2 Corinthians 1:3-4

I can't say I have ever entered into a time of sorrow thinking of comforting someone in the future. What about you? We journey through the hardships in life for two reasons—so God can refine us as we rely on him, and so he can use it to help others.

What is your most recent heartache? Where are you in your grief? Realize God wants to comfort you and heal you with his peace and presence. Have you spent time resting in his peace?

Are you ready for God to use your experience to bring his peace to someone else? It's okay if your answer is "not yet." As you walk through your valley, make a point of turning to him. Take note of Paul's description of God in verse three—the God of ___________________.

Wow! This same God loves you! Meditate for a moment on the word "all." What does it mean to you to know he is the God of all comfort who comforts all our afflictions?

Psalm 119:49-50

Where did the Psalmist find his hope in affliction?

What is your go-to scripture for hope and peace in your time of need?

Chapter 14

He Didn't Speak to Me in the Hall: Smoothing Out the Speed Bumps

That awkward moment when you try to explain your husband's single focus on Sunday mornings.

> Let your speech always be with grace, as though seasoned with salt, so that you will know how you should respond to each person. (Colossians 4:6)

"I think he's just about the rudest person I know."

"What kind of a preacher is not a people person?"

"It was like I wasn't even there!"

"Maybe I need to find another church. A church where the preacher actually speaks to me."

"I told him about my Aunt Jennie's surgery right before church started. Was he at the hospital? No!"

What do you suppose the average church member would say if I told her my husband has walked past me on a Sunday morning without speaking? Would she believe it?

It's true. I've been right there, looking just as pretty as a picture ... well, okay, I was standing there happy to have found matching shoes that morning ... and he walked right past me. Later that day, I asked him about it.

"Honey, why didn't you speak to me this morning when you walked by."

"I didn't walk past you this morning."

"Uh, yes, you did. On your way to the sanctuary. About twenty minutes before church started. Right past me."

"Oh. Well, I didn't see you. I'm sorry."

My husband is so focused on the upcoming worship hour on Sunday mornings, it is almost impossible for him to hear or see or think of anything else. As his wife and staff member, I try to protect his morning. I know if he is walking between his office and the sanctuary, his mind is thinking of one thing: worship. He has prepared all week. He has prepared the message and prepared his own heart. He is ready for worship.

Sunday morning is the worst time to try to get my husband's full attention. Whether it's me or a deacon or an adorable three-year-old, his mind is on worship.

He has often apologized from the pulpit for overlooking someone or forgetting a prayer request that was told to him minutes before worship. He has even requested folks give him prayer requests in writing.

Whether your husband is good at remembering conversations before he preaches, or he is like mine, chances are you have had to smooth ruffled feathers. It's awkward at best.

Recognizing no one likes to feel unimportant is an excellent beginning to making a difficult situation less uncomfortable.

I'm convinced most church members view us as the door to the preacher's attention. As the one who has an all-access pass, folks feel at ease letting us know what went wrong or where that preacher dropped the ball.

"Grace, grace, God's grace. Grace that will pardon and cleanse within." I read and reread this chapter, and all I can think of is God's grace. You and I have experienced God's grace. We experience it every day. And because he is generous with grace, we can be as well.

Repeat after me, "I'm so sorry he disappointed you," or "I promise he would never knowingly overlook you." After a heartfelt apology, you will often have an opportunity to help others understand their pastor a bit better. Without offering an excuse, you can explain his focus before he preaches.

People get upset for many reasons. It's crucial we keep from assuming every person who attends our church is in a growing relationship with Jesus. When we respond to complaints with grace, we disarm instead of fuel emotions. Even if confronted aggressively, grace will cover you.

I'm beating the same drum ... again ... spending the time with Jesus every day is the very key to being able to respond with grace. You and I can't do it on our own. We don't have enough grace in our entire bodies when we feel threatened or hurt. Without God's grace, our response would only cause trouble.

Grace, grace! God's grace! Isn't it great to know, he is never caught off guard by what people say or do? And isn't it pleasing to know, he will clothe us in his grace and help us respond in a godly way?

To the One who called my name and covered me with grace! Thank you for the special gift and calling of being a pastor's wife! I am humbled at the unique ways you choose to use me. Please, Father, forgive me when I try to do this life on my own. Forgive me when I walk out of the house spiritually naked. Please cover me with your grace today. Please help me to respond to the people in my path in a way that honors and glorifies you. Please open the doors that will allow me to share the great message of the great news of the gospel!

Thank you, LORD, for loving me every minute of every day. I want to be a vessel of your grace!

Sweet bites of wisdom: Being a pastor's wife is a high calling, but it is also a great responsibility and a great blessing. It is a gift from God. There are many demands, but the joys far outweigh the pressures. If you are a pastor's wife, it is of utmost importance that you know who you are in Christ and be focused on pleasing him first and foremost. Herbert Bayard Swope, the first recipient of the Pulitzer Prize for Reporting in 1917, has been quoted as saying, "I can't give you a sure-fire formula for success, but I can give you a formula for failure: try to please everybody all the time." When dealing with congregations, keep this in the front of your mind. ~ **Shirley Unrua**[20]

Pick up your fork: Colossians 4:2-6 and 1 Peter 4:7-11

Colossians 4:2-6

Does verse two give you a headache? When you read it, do you want to scream "I have no time for devoted prayer!"?

Sit a moment and breathe. Whatever season you are in—newlywed, small children, T-ball, and soccer, high school running, or empty nester—I know your plate is full and, more importantly, God knows. Remember that word *grace*? He is full of grace and love for you.

Being devoted to prayer doesn't necessarily mean you are seated in a closet with a towel over your head. No, being devoted in prayer is a beautiful part of the relationship with Jesus.

I pray and thank God for my meals. I pray in groups when I lead or teach. I pray with others when they ask me to. All those prayers are concluded with "in Jesus's name, Amen." I also pray all day. The conversation begins before I get out of bed and continues throughout the day. And never has an "Amen." It is the prayer that never ends.

Examine your prayer life. Are you devoted to prayer?

Verse three is beautiful. Paul requested prayer for open doors to speak the message of Christ. This is the way we should be praying for each other. How can a confrontation over your husband's "thoughtlessness" become an open door for the message of the good news?

Verses five speaks of walking in wisdom and making the most of the time we have. What is your initial response to verse six?

How does applying verse six to your personal circumstances help you know you can respond in a healing way to those who come to you with criticism?

1 Peter 4:7-11

We are, once again, called to be a people of prayer. How does this discipline prepare you for whatever may come your way today?

Print the last line in verse eight.

Apply that first to your own life. Aren't you super glad love covers a multitude of sins? I am! It goes back to grace. If God has enough love and forgiveness to cover my sins (and yours), surely I can respond in love to the person in front of me. It doesn't really matter if that person is looking to upset me or is genuinely wanting reconciliation and peace.

Everything we do or say is to glorify God. We can't do it alone. But when we are devoted to prayer, he will give us all the grace we need. So much so that it will spill out onto others.

Chapter 15

He Said What? From Your Lips to Their Ears.

Remembering what you say carries weight.

> For, THE ONE WHO DESIRES LIFE, TO LOVE AND SEE GOOD DAYS, MUST KEEP HIS TONGUE FROM EVIL AND HIS LIPS FROM DECEIT. (1 Peter 3:10)

The last time I checked, I was not covered with colorful feathers. I never sat on a perch. I don't squawk … much.

In other words, I have never been a parrot. I have my very own thoughts, ideas, dreams, and wishes.

And yet, there are some who think everything I say is repeated from a deeply secret conversation I had with my husband.

What? You don't like the color of the robes the choir wears?

Excuse me? You think the budget for the food ministry should be doubled?

Well, I never! You disagree with the youth pastor?

Translated: our pastor hates the choir, is a poor steward of God's money, and wishes our youth pastor would move on to another congregation.

A stretch? Maybe. Possible? Yes!

Often, but not often enough, my prayer is that God would protect me from myself. I don't ever want to be the source of conflict within the church family. I don't like to think about it very often, because it makes me nervous, but I recognize the potential I have for causing disruption. Satan has used many unsuspecting pastor's wives to bring a church to a place of chaos.

Please LORD, not me!

Here are a few safeguards I keep in place.

You remember the time with Jesus we've talked about a few times (cough, cough)? It always begins in those moments—the Scripture that teaches us, the Holy Spirit who holds us accountable, the prayer time that keeps our thoughts inline and clothes us with grace before we face the world. It is the best offense for knowing when to hold my tongue.

I am cautious when quoting my husband. I will quote something he said in a message like—what is down in the well comes up in the bucket. But to speak for him … uh … nope. Okay, wait. If asked if he likes banana pudding or hiking Mount Everest, those are easy answers! (Yes and no.) If I'm asked his opinion on something, the very best response is "I'm sure he would be happy to talk with you about this."

I have a close circle of friends who love me, warts and all. They have seen my shortcomings and have witnessed my failures. And they love me anyway. That is a wonderful gift! I'm unafraid to share my thoughts, ideas, and dreams with them. But do I speak for my husband even to good friends? No, I simply don't.

I've learned to keep my mouth closed more often than opening it. And guess what? I haven't exploded from internal combustion or even had to bite my tongue in two!

I realize this is a light-hearted approach to what could be a very serious conversation. But here's where the rubber hits the road. Just being mindful of my words, and even my wordless communication in the form of an eye roll or shoulder shrug keeps me safely on home plate.

We used to tell our children, just because you think it doesn't mean you have to say it.

It's true for me, and it's true for you. Our words carry the weight of who we are to our church family. Choose them carefully.

Hmmm, maybe I can choose to be a parrot after all! I can repeat James chapter three, Colossians chapter three, and Ephesians chapter five.

You are the Creator of life and words. Lord, I love you and want to honor you with my words. Please hold me close, so close I hear the whispers of your Holy Spirit, and I will know when to keep quiet and what words to use when it is time to speak.

Please protect my husband from the enemy. Stop the enemy from twisting truth and using his own words against him.

We want our words and actions to bring you honor. Please forgive us when we fail. Help us to rely on your word for instruction and strength.

Sweet bites of wisdom: "Whatever we've compared ourselves to—the ideal perfect wife that we all fall short of—we have to redefine it. We have to redefine what 'typical' is—not perfect, sharing in struggles and trying to grow and become a better woman in the world." **— Lori Wilhite**[21]

Pick up your fork: Read Mathew 15:1-20

What would fill my heart if I left it up to chance? '70's music from Sirius radio? Shameful humor from television sitcoms? Thoughts of myself and how others should treat me? Or worse?

Jesus's response to the elders caught then off guard. They were tied to their traditions. The teachings of man over the teachings of God.

If I want the words that come from my mouth to be pure, I need to pay close attention to what is in my heart.

The word defile means to spoil. If we truly want to be removed from the reality of a defiled heart, we must take care with how we choose to fill it.

After you have prayed over this passage, read it again. Linger at verses 8-9.

Is your heart far from God today?

Are you worshipping in truth or in vain?

No matter what weighs on you this moment, God's love and mercy hasn't changed. Fill your heart with godly things. Commit your heart and your words to his honor.

Banana Cream Pie

1 cup sugar

1/2 cup flour or 1/4 cup cornstarch

1/4 teaspoon salt

3 cups of milk

4 eggs, separated

3 tablespoons butter

1-1/2 teaspoons of vanilla extract

Bananas

1 9-inch baked pie shell

Combine sugar, flour, and salt in the top of a double boiler over medium heat. Gradually stir in milk. Cook and stir until thick and bubbly. Reduce heat and cook 2 minutes longer.

Remove from heat.

Beat the eggs yolks slightly. Gradually add 1 cup of hot mixture into yolks, stirring constantly. Return egg mixture to saucepan.

Place on low to medium heat until bubbling. Cook and stir 2 minutes.

Remove from heat and add vanilla and butter.

Place a generous number of sliced bananas on the bottom of the pie shell. Cover with creamed mixture.

Meringue

Beat egg whites until soft peaks form.

Add 1 teaspoon vanilla and slowly add 1/4 cup white sugar, continue to beat.

Beat until stiff peaks form.

Seal edges of pie as you cover it with the meringue. Bake at 350° until golden.

Chapter 16

I'm Only Human: Seeking Forgiveness for Failure

The biblical answer to messing up.

> He brought me up out of the pit of destruction, out of the miry clay, And He set my feet upon a rock making my footsteps firm. (Psalm 40:2-3)

They were in a bitter battle.

Three families.

Three perspectives.

Three sets of intense emotions.

There were moments when it appeared the fight might be ending, a lull so to speak. Just when we thought they would make amends and agree to disagree, something or someone would explode.

These three families were a part of the body of Christ, the local church. I was their pastor's wife, in my mid-twenties and they were all older than I.

I witnessed the bickering as it began to poison our sweet congregation, and yet, there was nothing I could do.

Almost nothing.

I read the beautiful story of Corrie Ten Boom; how she was able to forgive the men who murdered her family and stole all but her life. I read her words as she recalled the moment she looked into a congregation and into the face of the man who murdered her dear sister. She chose to forgive him.

If God could help Corrie forgive such horrendous pain and crime, God can help these families find healing through forgiving one another.

And then I did it.

The story was typed up, and three copies were made. Each was carefully folded and skillfully addressed. And without a word to my husband ... the pastor ... the letters were mailed. I felt a surge of satisfaction as I imagined each family opening the letter, reading it and rereading it. I smiled to myself as I pictured each one breaking down in a heap of "Forgive us, Lord." I patted myself on the back as I just knew the families would meet, talk, pray, hug, and all would be right in the world.

Did I mention I did not sign the letters?

I went my way and didn't think of it again. Well ... I wouldn't have thought of it again.

A few days later, after running errands, I walked into my husband's office to let him know I was home. He had no color in his face as he sat, glassy-eyed, staring at the wall.

"You're not going to believe it," he said. "Someone has anonymously sent letters to all three of the feuding families. The letters are copies of a Corrie Ten Boom story about forgiveness. Mr. Justified called first. He is angry. Later a call came from Mrs. Vinegar, and she is fuming."

I entered a suspended state of being. Swallowing and waiting to hear how this was going to end.

"Mr. You-Better-Fix-This called just a few minutes ago. He's planning to have the envelope analyzed. He might press charges. They are all blaming each other for the letter. I would never have believed it could get worse. But it got worse."

"Uh ... I, uh ... I s-s-sent the letters."

He just sat there and stared at me like he didn't hear me. I waited, feeling somewhat like a teenager who had been caught out past curfew.

"What should I do? I'm sorry. I just wanted to help. I thought it would help."

"You're going to have to go house to house and let them know the letters came from you. You can't talk to them over the phone. You need to go tonight, meet with them face to face and explain. Maybe they will calm down."

Praying and begging God to fix this mess I had created, I made my way to the first home.

Mr. Justified and his wife answered the door together and invited me in. I wasn't sure how I should approach the confession of my offense.

So, I cried. And I stumbled over every word. And the Justifieds were kind and forgiving.

Feeling somewhat fortified by the positive result, I headed over to the home of Mr. You-Better-Fix-This and his wife.

Enter. Sit. Replay. Cry. Stumble. Anger. Anger. Anger. A little bit of yelling and some more anger.

Whatever strength I had gained from the first stop had been washed away by the shame I experienced at the second. Acid indigestion had set in, and my head hurt.

I left that home with no forgiveness for what I had done.

Two down and one to go.

Mrs. Vinegar and her husband were glad to see me. I didn't quite cry this time—more like sniffles. Several tissues later, Mrs. Vinegar informed me all would have been okay had I just signed my name.

They were not as kind as the folks at my first stop, but not as cruel as the second. All in all, I had done what I could to correct my wrong.

There was one more forgiveness stop I had to make. My husband. He was still at his desk. There was a bit more color in his face. I explained that I never meant to cause him trouble; that I had always hoped to be the pastor's wife that supported ministry.

He was understanding and forgiving and thankful the snowball effect of anonymous mail had come to a stop.

As time went on, the issues resolved themselves.

What I learned that evening has helped me to this day, almost twenty-five years later.

The moral of this story has two parts:

If I can't sign my name, I won't send it on.

I am not the Holy Spirit.

Dear God, When I mess up and have no one to blame but myself, I am reminded of my frailties and shortcomings. Please keep my heart pure. Help me to truly rely on you for wisdom in all things.

Thank you for forgiving me and giving me a fresh, clean do-over. I recognize I cannot stay out of trouble on my own.

Thank you for your Church, for your people. Help me to love as you would have me love.

Amen

Sweet bites of wisdom: The pressure cooker of 24/7 ministry puts ours and others' sins and failures on display, but it also puts on display the grace of God that allows us to receive and give daily forgiveness and mercy. It turns out to be true that "blessed are the poor in spirit." Blessed are those who have nothing and know it, because that is the way to receive everything from our faithful Savior Jesus. To the extent that being a pastor's wife forces me to rely on Jesus for everything – that is a great grace.
—Barbara Miller Juliani[22]

Pick up your fork: Hebrews 12:1-17

I was only seven or eight years old. I knew my mother told me to stay out of the old barn. She said there was nothing to see. She explained the barn didn't belong to us. She cautioned the building wasn't safe.

But what is a curious little girl to do? I ventured in and looked around. I was fascinated by the sight of the sun's rays streaming through the old walls. I enjoyed the smell of old hay and rusty tools. And I wondered what I would hear if old barns could tell stories of memories past.

My disobedience didn't hit me until I squeezed from the shadows of the barn back into summer's bright light. I looked back at the barn and noticed its sway. Was this what my mother meant by unsafe? Or did she mean the hornet's nest that was nestled in the eaves?

Mom was waiting for me. She watched as I walked toward the house. I didn't have a good defense for my choice to disobey. Discipline was waiting.

How often does sin sing the same song to me? Luring me with the idea of a harmless adventure or some secret delight?

Consider Hebrews 12 as God so lovingly informs us of the key to stopping ourselves from following sin's call.

Print the phrases in verses 1-2 that call us to action. The words that almost give us a step by step plan of action to be able to escape sin.

Verses 3-13 remind me of facing the discipline waiting as my mom watched me walk toward the house. She disciplined because she loved me. How much greater is God's love? Recall his discipline in your life. How long did you wait before repenting and clearing the air between you?

Verses 14-17 is perfect instructions for each day. How will you pursue peace with everyone? That no root of bitterness will spring up?

How will you share the good news of the gospel of Christ?

Chapter 17

The Church Is Messy

Remembering heaven is the only place that doesn't get messy.

> Therefore let us draw near with confidence to the throne of grace, so that we may receive mercy and find grace to help in time of need. (Hebrews 4:16)

Twice a year, we invite the people of the church to come out on a Saturday for a cleaning day. It's always great to see so many folks give up a chunk of Saturday to polish, trim, sanitize, and pressure wash God's house inside and out. Especially heartwarming is to see families there. I love when Moms and Dads model what they want their kids to grow up doing.

One particular work day as I did my part, I thought of how messy church is. I'm not talking about the wadded-up tissue under the pew or the "quarterly" from Spring of 2010. Side-note—many years ago, I had a friend who would strategically place a candy wrapper on the floor during worship so she could see if anyone had cleaned when she returned the following Sunday. Are you rolling your eyes? I know, right?

Back to the point, the church is messy. Perhaps my friend of old illustrates the point. The Church is not the building—the Church is people. The Church is people who get together, hopefully often, to learn, worship, fellowship, grow, and take care of one another.

We have a unique bird's-eye view of the Church. As a pastor's wife, we get to witness and be a part of the Church at its best. It is also very much a part of our lives when the Church struggles.

We (meaning people who profess Jesus as Savior) are all on our own journey to know him better and love him more. We all have our own baggage. Some of us learned a long time ago how to give everything to God and allow him to use life's hurts to make us more like him. Others of us aren't there yet.

And we're all messy.

We get our feelings hurt.

We struggle with forgiveness.

We misunderstand one another.

We make assumptions.

We feel insecure.

We want to make a difference and often aren't sure how.

Yes, the Church is messy.

Even so, I wouldn't walk away from this beautiful family for anything. I'm glad we are all in this together. We can all say, "He's still workin' on me," and maybe give each other a bit more room to be imperfect.

May I speak to you from the heart of one Pastor's wife to another? Don't be too hard on those around you who wear their baggage like a backpack. Be kind and show grace. Tomorrow you might be the one dragging a heavy bag around.

I always enjoy the Sunday after the Saturday workday. It's great to get up in the morning, put my best foot forward, and go to church. I love walking into a room that shines and smells lemony fresh!

I hope God uses me to help carry someone's bag. After all, that's what makes us the Church. And we need to remember until we all get to heaven, Church is messy.

Father, I'm thankful for the Church, for the people who get together to worship you. For those who serve and do your work in so many ways.

I'm even thankful for the messes. They remind me of the frailty of life and your power to clean up the messes.

I admit, sometimes I don't feel much like bearing another's burden. Sometimes I want to dodge and weave through the grocery store to avoid "that" person. Please forgive me and give me a heart of compassion. Remind me, it's not my job to fix people, but it is my place to be available to your call to befriend.

Thank you for the people along the way who have helped me with my baggage.

Sweet bites of wisdom: Maybe Paul was talking about being a pastor's wife when he said, "I have become all things to all men, that I might by all means save some." So I'll be the Conversation Killer and the People Rolodex and the Nameless Person if it also means I get to be Disciple Maker and Counselor and Lover of People.

Paul said it best: "Now this I do for the gospel's sake.

It's a pretty good gig. ~ **Christine Hoover**[23]

Pick up your fork: Ephesians 4:17-32

It seems we are living in a constant state of outrage, uproar, offense, and rebuke. I get seriously worn out to read or watch the news. How did we get here?

If seeing the world rolling in turmoil isn't pitiful enough, that same turmoil has inched into the Body of Christ. Unrest and dissatisfaction.

There's only one explanation. We've lost our focus. We've placed our eyes on ourselves and have forgotten what being the body of Christ means.

God has supplied more than enough instructions for us. I love the practical and godly guidelines given in Ephesians 4.

As you study this passage, ask God to cause words and phrases to jump off the page and cause personal discomfort in the areas you need to give to him for refining.

Write a prayer using verses 25-32 as your foundation. Commit to God to do your part to strengthen the family. Ask God to show you specifics of what he has planned for you.

Ah, the body of Christ. She is a gift to be treasured.

Chapter 18

Checkmate: Remembering the True Enemy

People are not your enemy. Relying on the Bible through the battles.

> Be of sober spirit, be on the alert. Your adversary, the devil, prowls around like a roaring lion, seeking someone to devour. (1 Peter 5:8)

I had only known her for less than twenty-four hours.

She was younger than me.

It was years ago, but we have kept in touch.

"Shelley, you cannot allow this pain to cause bitterness to take root in your heart. Bitterness will ruin you. Remember who the real enemy is. Your enemy is Satan, not the people he has used to hurt you. Give your pain to God; he will use it in your life. I am praying for you."

It was the only retreat for pastor's wives I have ever attended. I carried with me the pain of betrayal, lies spread by people who were supposed to be my friends, and abandonment. I felt abandoned by people I expected would be in my life through eternity. I had already celebrated weddings and births with them in my mind. We had, in reality, cried together as we faced cancer, divorce, and death. And now they were gone. They believed what they heard and walked out of my life. Unbelievably, there were those who perpetuated the rumors once they left.

My heart was broken. My husband was crushed.

How could this happen?

What had we done that was so terrible? Had we committed a sin that brought the wrath of God? My husband and I spent many hours praying and searching. We knew we were not perfect people. We knew we, like any other person, were capable of making mistakes.

We also knew we had not done the horrific things we were accused of. As we waded through a sea of difficult Sundays and impossible Mondays, we were stunned with each new revelation.

We were blessed by mentors in our lives. Godly people who gave us godly advice and prayed for us. God provided shelter during the storm, but we still had to live through it all.

At the time of the retreat, I looked at those who spread rumors as my enemy. I sat quietly among a little less than two dozen pastor's wives. The guest speaker taught about using the gifts God had given each of us. She provided a hands-on way to record our dreams and steps to realizing them in God's time.

The second day of the retreat, she opened the floor for discussion. I, along with several others, shared my pain. Some faces stared back in shock. Some had the look of fear. Many cried. I listened to the women who spoke. They said serving the church was wearing them down. Their marriages were suffering. Their children were caught in the fray. They longed for normalcy. They longed for family. They longed for life.

At the end of the last session, several of us went to the cottage of two who traveled to the retreat together. I wasn't sure why I was going. I wanted to go back to my room and bury my head under the blankets.

I stepped in and immediately noticed their friendship. "How wonderful for them," I thought. We talked a bit, ate a bit, and laughed a lot. When I got ready to leave, Jennifer stood up.

That's when she spoke to my bleeding heart. When she reminded me who my enemy was, she also brought to light the nature and power of God. She reminded me I had a choice to make. If I chose bitterness, I also chose to remove God from the throne in my life. I would render him powerless in me. God and bitterness do not live together.

If I chose forgiveness, God's power to work in me and through me would be unleashed. The real enemy, the one who wanted to destroy my family and my husband, also wanted to destroy the church.

I went back to my room that night and had a most wonderful time of soul searching and worship. Confession for focusing my anger on people. Admission for being angry with God for allowing it all. And praise, so much praise. Praise because I believe his promise to work in all things.

Praise because I believe he is faithful to complete what he began in me—in my husband, in our children, in his church—faithful beyond measure.

And I asked him to take away any bitterness that had moved in to stay.

Satan uses people to accomplish destruction. Some folks don't even know they are tools in Satan's grasp. Some folks don't care.

People are not your enemy. You and I have one enemy. Satan.

I wish I could tell you that weekend worked a miraculous change in the battle we faced. It did not. We faced heartache and difficulties for quite some time. Even now, many years later, we continue to deal with reminders of what happened to our sweet church family and us.

But when reminded, we have a choice to make. We can choose bitterness and anger, or we can choose to remember who the real enemy is and trust God to be God.

> *It's me again, Lord. Sometimes I feel so trapped by my own emotions. I want to understand the whys and hows of this life. I confess I want to strike back. Eye for an eye. I want to run away. I want to hide. I want to speak my mind.*
>
> *And yet, I know that is not what you have planned for me. I cannot separate my enemy from the people he uses. I cannot, but you can.*
>
> *I give my weak thoughts and misgivings to you. I give you my hurt. And, even more difficult, I give my husband to you. I trust you to work in him and to bring good from all the sorrow.*
>
> *I give my sweet, sweet church family to you. The little children who don't know yet that such evil exists, the senior adults who are so very faithful, and the ones who I once looked at enemies.*
>
> *May you be glorified!*

Sweet bites of wisdom: Cling to the faithful. Satan's biggest scheme is to attack my thoughts and shoot lies that say, "You are in this alone, nothing is secure, you're fighting a battle that will never be won." He also throws a heap of hopelessness on the fact that no matter where we go or who we minister to its the same broken tune. The truth is, that's not reality and it is very much a lie. You aren't alone in this. You aren't unlovable. And what you are fighting for is absolutely worth it no matter how jacked up it may be. There are those within your church that faithfully and lovingly care for you. They are there each week. They may even be easy to gloss over because they aren't the ones causing a rift or saying too much. They serve faithfully. They really do you love you, and you need to remind yourself (and your husband) of this. Furthermore, you have others beside you in the trenches. I love Paul's word's in Philippians where he says that "We stand firm, side by side, for the sake of the Gospel." You aren't in this battle alone so don't try to go lone ranger. Don't bottle it up inside. Pray, Share, Wrestle with others who are faithfully fighting for and beside you. **—Jacki C. King**[24]

Pick up your fork: 1 John 3

There is no greater pain than the pain of seeing your husband betrayed by a staff member or by someone attending church. There is a lonely kind of sorrow that tries to take over.

We grieve when the church family fights, splits, and gossips. We are pained when friends walk away.

We are tempted to lash back. But, if we did, we would not be able to engage the true enemy. Nor should we try.

Satan has used both willing and unknowing "church" people for centuries to battle against God. Why would you and I think our lives would be free from it?

1 John chapter 3 begins with encouragement as we are reminded of how great the Father's love is for us. What is your response to his love?

Wade through the chapter, spending extra time in prayer. Praise God for his great love and provision against our enemy.

Why was the Son of God revealed?

How are God's children as well as those who belong to Satan made evident?

How do we know love?

What is his command in verse 23?

How do we know Christ remains in us?

If we know his spirit dwells in us, we can also know he will fight the battles for us. Our job is to continue to grow in grace and knowledge. To do what it right and keep his commandments.

Your Life is My Business: They Don't Own You

Our church was most generous and gave us a two-month sabbatical. The Saturday before our first Sunday back, I did what every good pastor's wife does … I had my hair done.

I have gone to the same "hair guy" (as he refers to himself) for over twenty-eight years. I trusted him to the point I seldom asked for anything. I sat down, and he worked his magic.

Sometimes the shade of my decidedly red hair was a bit on the bronzish side. Other times it was more strawberry-blonde than the deep auburn I preferred.

This day was no different than any other before. I sat down, we small talked. He mixed up his potion and did his thing.

I got in my car and checked the mirror. "OH, MY WORD! I'M AN EGGPLANT!"

Yup, my hair was purple. PURPLE!

My husband tried to tell me it was fine. "It'll be okay," he said.

I sent a picture to my sisters, and they wanted to know if I also got a tattoo!

The next morning, I checked the mirror thinking maybe I had just had a crazy dream. Nope. I was still an eggplant.

I decided to embrace the purple. My church family had not seen me in two months, would they even notice the new color? (Yeah, I really wondered that!)

What followed throughout the morning was actually a lot of fun. Kids and the twenty-somethings loved the color. Some stared as they welcomed me back. Others wondered out loud what happened. I joked this was my sabbatical hair.

The color has grown on me. I confess—I like it!

This long story is told to make one quick point. You belong to God and are not owned by your congregation. It's okay to listen to their suggested instructions on how to raise your children, what kind of clothes you should wear, what area of ministry suits you best, and … well … yes, what color your hair should be.

But when all is said and done, remember you are a child of the King. It's okay to be comfortable in your own skin … and hair.

Best Sugar Cookies Ever

2 sticks of BUTTER
1-1/2 cups white sugar
2 eggs
1 teaspoon pure vanilla extract
2-3/4 cups all-purpose flour
1/2 teaspoon salt
1/2 teaspoon baking powder
1/2 teaspoon cinnamon

Cream butter and sugar until fluffy.
Add eggs and vanilla extract. Mix until combined.
Sift together dry ingredients and add to wet ingredients.
Mix well and chill in the refrigerator at least one hour.

Roll to 1/4 inch thickness and cut to desired shapes.
Bake 375° for 8-10 minutes.

Icing:
1 cup confectioners' sugar
1 tablespoon softened butter
1/2 teaspoon vanilla extract
Small amount of milk (this is up to you and how thick or thin you like your icing)

Chapter 19

She's Putting on Weight: Yes, You Can Learn to Smile at What They Say

Responding in a kind matter to those who are thoughtless.

> But the wisdom from above is first pure, then peaceable, gentle, reasonable, full of mercy and good fruits, unwavering, without hypocrisy. (James 3:17)

The warm sun brightened the afternoon as we enjoyed watching our son play Little League baseball. His little sister and brother sat nearby entertained by small toys from home.

And then it happened.

She walked up with an inviting smile covering her face.

"Hey, Shelley."

"Hi."

"Um, are you pregnant?"

"No. Just fat."

"Oh, good! 'Cause I thought to myself 'oh laaaaawd, Shelley better not be pregnant again!'"

And then she walked away.

Just. Like. That.

Confession time—I immediately began to wonder how quickly I could have another baby. That would show her ...

The thoughts that followed spiraled downward. My cheeks burned, and embarrassment crawled all over me.

And then I got angry.

How rude!

Who does she think she is?

Like she's perfect or something …

Of course, you know, I didn't say any of this out loud. Instead, the thoughts swirled around in my heart for days.

I wish I could tell you it didn't last. Truth be told, I held it against her for a long time.

I found myself consumed with body image.

Do I look pregnant?

How could I let myself go like this?

What a disappointment.

I didn't pray about it. I didn't read my Bible. I relied on my own perspective and somehow thought the end result would be a good thing. The worst part was assuming the end result would honor my God. And in the meantime, I avoided her.

If I could have a do-over ...

"Um, are you pregnant?"

"No. Just carrying a little weight from my last baby."

"Oh, good! 'Cause I thought to myself 'oh laaaaawd, Shelley better not be pregnant again!'"

Smile.

"Shew! No, not anytime soon. But I'd appreciate it if you pray for me as I try to eat right."

Perhaps if I had relied on the wisdom from above, my response would have been pure, peaceable, and gentle. Not only toward my friend in my thoughts but also toward myself.

The word intreat in James 3:17 is the old English word for entreat and means to ask for earnestly. God's wisdom is easy to request. God's wisdom is full of mercy and good fruits. God's wisdom is void of partiality and hypocrisy—and there for the asking.

Let's face it. Thoughtless and downright mean comments are going to happen. We can be prepared for such moments by asking earnestly for God's wisdom. We can purpose in our hearts to respond with grace whether we are being criticized or complimented.

A couple of years later, I sat in the warm sun watching our son play ball as baby number four kicked her way into my heart. There was plenty of room for her there, for I no longer held any animosity for my friend.

Author of all Wisdom, thank you for your patience with us as we learn to rely on your wisdom and not our own. We want our response to all people to be pure, peaceable, and gentle. We recognize we cannot do it without you. Please forgive us for trying to please you on our own. As your First Ladies, please cover us with your grace and keep us ever mindful of your mercy not only in our lives but in the lives of our church family.

Sweet bites of wisdom: We may not always see it, or feel it, we might forget it's there at times, or even wonder if he's left us to fend for ourselves in the heat of hard situations of life. But his protection is real. He doesn't, he can't, forget us or ignore us. If we belong to him, his love is too great to leave us on our own. **—Debbie McDaniel**[25]

Pick Up Your Fork: Matthew 5-7.

Matthew 5-7

Imagine in your mind's eye, the people gathered around Jesus on a mountainside, listening to the words of wisdom. I had had the privilege of traveling to Israel on several occasions. My favorite place is the Garden of the Beatitudes. It is the perfect setting for Jesus to have taught so many at one time. Place yourself there as you read. Allow his teaching to permeate your heart. Highlight the passages that jump off the page at you. Remember, your goal is not to become the perfect wife of a pastor. No. Your goal is to submit to Christ's lead and become more like him each day.

Matthew 7:24

This verse begins Jesus's closing illustration to the Sermon on the Mount which began in chapter 5. List practical ways you will act on his words the next time you are faced with unfair or unkind circumstances.

Chapter 20

I Cannot Be Your Friend: There's a Reason You Are Lonely

> For it is not an enemy who reproaches me,
> Then I could bear *it*;
> Nor is it one who hates me who has exalted himself against me,
> Then I could hide myself from him.
> But it is you, a man my equal,
> My companion and my familiar friend;
> We who had sweet fellowship together
> Walked in the house of God in the throng.
> (Psalm 55:12-14)

I was twenty-three years old. We had a baby, and I was barely three months pregnant with baby number two. New to the church family, we were just beginning to get our bearings.

She was one of the first people I met in the new church. She was my age and not yet married but engaged. We got along great, and I was thankful for a friend.

The friendship lasted about two years. She called one morning. And before I knew it, the conversation was over, and I stood in my kitchen, stunned.

She said it was just too hard to be my friend. She just couldn't do it any longer.

I had no idea "church politics" were involved. It was then that I began to learn there are different types of church members.

There are those who genuinely want more Jesus. They are there to learn, grow, and serve.

There are those who haven't quite figured it out yet, but they are interested and want to understand God's plan.

There are the social clubbers. They are there because that's just what you do.

And, there are those who want to be big fish in a small pond. They want to run the church, make big decisions, and be sure they have their way.

Little did I know then, my friend who found it too hard to remain friends was engaged to be married into a family of little fish who wanted to be big fish.

She found herself at a table where folks often had the preacher for lunch, not as an invited guest but as the topic of conversation. She had a choice to make. She could speak up for our friendship and alienate her future in-laws, or she could separate herself from me.

Not long after our friendship ended, the trouble between my husband and the "little fish" began.

That was many years ago, and since then God has sent some true-blue people into my life. I am blessed to have a circle of friends who have walked through fire beside me.

It can feel like we are walking a tightrope, this search for friendship. We cannot see the future or read the mind and heart of one who is befriending us.

So what can we do?

We can listen. Pay close attention to the topic of conversation. Does your new friend enjoy tearing others down? Telling stories that begin with "I heard"? Dreaming up accusations? The old saying "if they do it with you, they will do it to you" is amazingly accurate. Don't yoke yourself with someone who practices this kind of "friendship."

Wade in slowly. Don't bare your soul to people who have not proven themselves faithful. A sign of a loyal friend is one who doesn't need details to pray for you. A faithful friend is concerned with what she can do to help you grow closer to Jesus. A faithful friend is not selfish in the friendship but understands the give and take of a growing relationship.

And best of all, we can ask God for the wisdom to know the difference between genuine friendship and a fishing expedition. He has protected me on more than one occasion from such a "friend." God has given me what I describe as a catch in my spirit, a clear message of "keep it superficial." There have been times when I didn't quite understand why I needed to keep this person at arm's length, but soon enough the real motivation for friendship surfaced.

It almost seems ridiculous that friendship within the church could be such a minefield. But when we think of the war we fight, and the fact souls are a stake, it only makes sense that our enemy would use friendships as a weapon.

Giver of every good and perfect thing, I know you created me to be a social being. I have a need for true friends around me. Thank you for the gentle guiding of your Holy Spirit. Thank you for bringing people into my life who want to see me succeed. Thank you for speaking truth to me and helping me make wise choices with my closest friends.

Help me to be the kind of friend that brings others closer to you. Keep me humble, genuine, dependent on you, and true to your word.

Protect me from myself. You know sometimes I find myself talking too much and not listening enough.

I love you, LORD! I love you!

Sweet bites of wisdom: I've had very close friends that were in my circle that for one reason or another have left the church and every time it hurts. Those times are always painful, but it doesn't cause me to stop living life and stop investing in other friendships. So my words of wisdom for pastor's wives is to remember that ministry is all about people. You have to have a soft heart toward people, but a guarded heart when it comes to who you let get close to you. Also, don't let friendships that end painfully cause you to become cynical toward people. You have to learn to walk in forgiveness and choose to extend unconditional Christ like love toward all people. **—Martha Fry**[26]

Pick up your fork: Proverbs 13:20 and Psalm 41:9

Friendship can be a minefield. We have a longing for friends and at the same time, we fear friendship.

Proverbs 13:20

This verse is a great starting point for any friendship. Take your time before forming a close friendship. Watch and listen. What are the signs of a wise friend?

Here are a few questions to answer:

Does my friend gossip?

Am I expected to reveal confidential information?

Do we pray together?

Does my friend encourage me with Scripture?

Have I prayed for wisdom to know if this person is a true and godly friend?

Psalm 41:9

This verse reminds us we are not alone when facing the betrayal of a friend.

What safeguards do you have in place to keep from attaching yourself precariously to the wrong friends?

How does your daily walk and quiet time help you when forming friendships?

Chapter 21

I Always Feel Like Somebody's Watching Me: Well, That's Because They Are

You are an example to others whether you like it or not. Make the best of the opportunities.

> You are the salt of the earth; but if the salt has become tasteless, how can it be made salty again? It is no longer good for anything, except to be thrown out and trampled underfoot by men. (Matthew 5:13)

I found the small, pretty box at my office door. Inside the envelope with the box, there was a beautiful, handwritten letter. There was no signature at the end.

She wrote of what she had seen as she watched my relationship with my daughter. She said she hoped and prayed her relationship with her daughter would be as sweet. She quoted Scripture for being the fragrance of Christ in a lost and dying world.

Inside the box was a lovely, small perfume bottle that looks like a miniature "I Dream of Jeannie" bottle. This unknown-to-me mom gave me a precious gift. It was not the sweet letter or the beautiful bottle, although they are dear to me, and I have them still. It was the reminder of who I am in Christ. It was a reminder of the gift he gave me when he made me Mrs. Pastor. In giving me the title of pastor's wife, he gave me a unique way to minister to and care for the women in my life.

At first, I was a nervous wreck at the thought of my parenting skills or lack thereof being on display. I knew I was only doing the best I could, and just like so many, I was on a learning curve. Learning as I go.

Even so, it had not occurred to me before I read this precious note that others were watching my parenting. If she had signed her letter, I am sure I would have gone to her right away and begged her not to pattern herself after me in any way.

There are other ways you and I are on display.

During church business meetings.

In the grocery store with the kids—they are watching what's in the buggy as much as what's going on outside it.

At the movie theatre.

In the bookstore.

On date night with our honey-love.

It's true. You and I are being watched.

Let's think about that for a moment. Here we face yet another choice. We can choose paranoia, worry, or anxiety. We can decide to try to seclude and hide. Or, we can choose to live the life God intended.

We don't have to overcomplicate it. We don't need to put more pressure on ourselves or our children. We can do the very same thing God required of Adam and Eve, Abraham and Sarah, Moses and Zipporah, and Timothy's mother and grandmother! God's requirements have been the same since the dawn of time. What does he require of us? Act justly, love faithfulness, and walk humbly with him.

It is freeing to know his requirements are the same for of us as they are any other believer. Whether you have no children or fifteen. Whether we shop at the mom and pop grocery or the specialized health food store. Whether we sing from the hymnal or contemporary Christian music.

Act justly. Treat people with love and kindness.

Love faithfulness. Being faithful to God is a priority.

And walk humbly with God. Learn, grow, serve, and let your light shine for him.

What matters most to me is what God thinks of me. Not what Sister Sally or Brother Bill have to say. I want to stand before God with clean hands and a pure heart. I don't have to be concerned with being watched if I'm living to honor God with my life.

My husband and I often talk about what we would change if we had it all to do over again. And we are thankful, in spite of our many flaws, God has gifted us with incredible kids. We are thankful he has grown us from the young babies we were in the beginning to where we are now.

Most of all, we are thankful he isn't finished with us yet. We have more to learn and more to accomplish for him.

That beautiful little bottle of fragrant oil? I still have it as a reminder of who I am in Christ. A reminder to me I have choices to make every day. I choose to be the fragrance of Christ. I need and want God to hold me accountable for who I am in him.

Do you always feel like someone's watching you? Well, that's because they are. And it's okay!

> *To the One who sees and knows all, I give my day to you. Please keep me more mindful of your watchful eye than that of others. Help me to remember that if pleasing you with my thoughts, words, and actions is what matters most to me, I have nothing to fear from others.*
>
> *Please protect me from bringing shame to your name. Keep me ever near, so when others look at me, they see less me and more you. Control my mouth and my attitude. Control my thoughts and my actions.*
>
> *I love you, Lord, and want to honor you above all else.*

Sweet bites of wisdom: There is no such thing as a cookie cutter pastor's wife. Each place of worship, each home, has its own flavor or atmosphere and focus. Some churches specialize in prayer and intercession, not only because the pastors love this area of ministry—they are called by God to intercede and pray.

Other churches specialize in excellent worship. Those churches will attract people who have those needs and will set others free who are captive and do not know how to enter into those special ministries. (this applies to witnessing, helping less fortunate, etc.)

Giving yourself permission to embrace your strengths builds confidence and creates a world of thanksgiving and joy, forgiveness and understanding. The fruits of the spirit are abundant in those who are filled with praise and worship. Truth sets captives free ... and frankly, is a whole lot more fun!
—Shannon Parish[27]

Pick up your fork: Romans 12:2 and Psalm 71:1-8

Romans 12:2

When he tells a joke in his message, many heads turn to see if I am laughing. When he uses me as an illustration and I am helping in the nursery, people rush to tell me what he said. When our children were young, I was criticized for disciplining and for not disciplining enough. I'm guessing you are shaking your head in a been-there-done-that kind of way.

So, friend—how you doin'? Are you bearing up under the watchful eyes?

May I encourage you with what you already know. Stop by Romans 12:2 for a minute. I've been searching to see if it applies to us alone or to all believers (wink, wink).

Instructions on living a godly life are the same for all believers. So, exhale and find a place to rest. Renew your mind so you may discern what is God's good and perfect will.

Psalm 71

Then hop on over to Psalm 71. Enjoy these verses as the Psalmist places his trust in God. Have you made God your only refuge? When you feel the pressure of people, do you run to the Father for safety? Have you found him to be your rock when you need an unshakable, immovable fortress?

Seriously, it's okay that people are watching you. You don't need to worry about what they see if you are placing your trust in God alone. Rely on him to be your daily guide. Listen to his still small voice. Submit to his lead.

You'll be just fine.

CHAPTER 22

My First Friend: Honest Above All

It takes years to build this kind of friendship.

> Truthful lips will be established forever, But a lying tongue is only for a moment. (Proverbs 12:19)

Three young children and a brand-new church home. We knew we were "home" from the moment we walked through the doors. We were ready to love this new church family. And prepared to be loved.

She invited me to bring the kids and join her for a picnic at the park. My guard was up. I wasn't ready to make close friends yet. I wanted to settle in and learn about my new surroundings. I needed time to feel comfortable enough to bloom where God planted us.

She invited, and even though I felt great caution, the children and I met her at the park.

This new friend was unlike anyone I had ever met before. There was no pretense. She was who she was, take her or leave her.

She laughed.

She played with the kids.

She told me stories.

She was the real deal.

Years into our friendship, she told me how she felt my hesitance that day in the park. She said she could look at me and tell I had been hurt and wasn't ready to open myself up to a relationship again.

Even so, she became my first friend. We've known each other nearly three decades now. Our friendship has come and gone in seasons. Seasons of much time together and seasons of time passing without a word. Seasons of shared sorrows and seasons of shared joy.

But always, no matter what season we seem to be in, she can be counted on to be my faithful friend. She is unafraid to speak the truth to me, even when she knows it will hurt to hear. She doesn't tell me what I want to hear, she tells me the truth.

She has, on more than one occasion, said "Shell, are you okay? Sit down and talk to me." I like that she calls me "Shell." She's the only one.

What a rare jewel she is in my life.

She reminds me often that her door is always open. And in some of my darkest nights, just knowing that door is open has brought me much comfort. I have imagined showing up, and without a word, crying for an hour or so before going home. She's that kind of friend. She's a safe place for me.

She is also an example for me of the unconditional love of Christ. I've watched her open her home to many. She reminds me of the innkeeper in the parable of the Good Samaritan. She opens the door and welcomes the lonely. She opens her home and welcomes the wandering. She opens her heart and embraces the friendless.

She is no stranger to loss. She has allowed God to use the pain in her life to make her more like Christ. Instead of growing bitter, her pain has pushed her forward. It drives her to love others without judgment.

We laugh when we remember how unsure she was of Tommy. She loved me from the word go, but the preacher? Not so much. Their friendship took a bit more time. She loves him faithfully now.

She is bold in standing up for what she believes in.

She cries easily. Apologizes for her tears when she shouldn't.

Sometimes puts her mouth in drive before putting her brain in gear and is supremely embarrassed by it—a quality that is endearing to me because her heart is not devious. No, her heart breaks if she thinks she has hurt someone.

I know how very blessed I am by God. He gave me this first friend. She is my forever friend.

Look around you. Is your forever friend waiting for you to discover her? Perhaps she is a grandmother, waiting for you to stop by for a visit. Maybe she is your age and would love an invite to lunch. Could she be younger than you, in a season of life you survived? You can tell her to trust

God in this season. Can you tell stories of God's faithfulness and encourage her along the way?

Forever friends aren't made overnight or without effort. And you know what, it's okay to have more than one. I have taken what I have learned from her and have applied to my life. I want to be that first friend of the woman in my church who has the guarded look in her eyes.

What about you? Who is your forever first friend? And how has it made you better?

Dear God, it's so easy to become preoccupied with the negatives in life. Easy to focus on friendships gone wrong or that time I was mistreated. Forgive me, Father, for refusing to look at all the wonderful gifts of friendship you have provided.

Help me to look for the one who needs a friend. For the one who thinks there is no such thing as a true friend. Help me to be that friend, not just to the one in need, but to the women in our congregation. I know I can't be everyone's best friend. I know I must be wise with what I say to people. I also know, you can use me to befriend the unfriendly.

I want to be a picture of your grace. I want to be a friend, a true friend, to the women in my life. I trust you to work in me and through me.

Sweet bites of wisdom: Realize that you need friends to become the woman God wants you to be. Don't distance yourself from the women in your own congregation and limit yourself to friendships with other pastors' wives. Develop friendships with women in your same church family who share your life and purpose. Don't worry about appearing to show favoritism by forming friendships with some women in your church and not others; know that it's natural to be drawn to some people over others. Just be sure to be friendly to everyone, regardless of how close you are to them. **—Whitney Hopler**[28]

Pick up your fork: 2 Corinthians 8:21 and Colossians 3:9-10

2 Corinthians 8:21

This verse is pulled from a passage where Paul tells of the excellent care he and others took in keeping up with the gifts given by the people. It was necessary for Paul to take precautions so there would be no question as to their integrity. The friendship between Paul and Titus is evident in this passage.

With your focus on verse 21, what steps do you personally have in place to help you as you choose each day to live a life that is pleasing to God? What measures do you use to remain a person of truth?

Colossians 3:9-10

Previous verses remind us we are new creations, in new bodies, and therefore, we must put away our habits of old.

Paul gives the commandment to remain truthful with each other because we have put off our old ways.

Write a prayer using verses from Colossians chapter 3. Include confession for any words you have spoken that are from the "old nature." Ask the Holy Spirit to hold you so firmly you know before you talk if your words will honor him. Rely on him to give you the integrity you need to be a woman of grace-filled truth.

Chapter 23

Monkey in the Middle: Ministering to the Hatfields and McCoys

The difficult task of being the pastor's wife to all people during conflict.

> Thus says the Lord, "Preserve justice and do righteousness, For My salvation is about to come And My righteousness to be revealed." (Isaiah 56:1)

In case you are of a generation unaware of the Hatfields and McCoys, allow me to bring you up to speed. In short, they are two Appalachian families, embroiled in a feud that reaches so far back they don't even know what they are fighting about.

When I was a little girl, I was introduced to the Hatfields and McCoys as portrayed by Fred Flintstone and friends. It was an amusing cartoon that left me wondering why on earth two groups of people would use so much energy hating each other.

I have found myself wedged in between feuding parties. I would never choose to go there on my own. It has sort of happened by default.

I would listen to the case presented by first one side and then the other. I felt somewhat dirty—like I had betrayed everyone because I listened to complaints. It's a trapped feeling.

If you stay in one church long enough, your path will cross a feud. How do you love on and minister to people who are on the outs with each other?

It is possible, although never comfortable.

I have made statements like this: "I want you to know that I love so and so as much as I love you. I am her pastor's wife and friend, just as I am your pastor's wife and friend. Please understand, I am not going to do or say anything that would harm these friendships. I am praying for you to be able to resolve your difference. I am praying for God to be glorified through this."

One of two things happen. Either that is our final conversation on the matter (because some folks just want me to get in the mud with them and when I won't, well, I am no longer needed), or we are able to agree to go to God for what is required to bring reconciliation.

Don't allow yourself to get caught up in a tug-o-war. It can happen in the blink of an eye.

How can you keep from getting stuck in between a rock and a hard place? I bet you can guess!

It always goes back to your time with God. I love the Proverbs passage that cautions us to look to God and not trust our own impulse or understanding. I tried this once, okay several times. This relying on my own understanding thing. I was caught in the middle of angry parents, each blaming the other for their children's hurt feelings. Each couple had a daughter. The daughters were friends … until they were no longer friends. In my own great wisdom, I invited both couples to sit down with me and work it out. I did not pray about it. I just went with it.

Can I tell you it was disastrous? Oh, my, was it ever a disaster. In the end, both families left the church. Instead of a big group hug, as I had envisioned, it ended with crying moms and angry dads.

I learned a valuable lesson that day. I am not Dr. Phil! I learned an even more valuable lesson. God is the only one who can smooth the wrinkles in relationships. It is my place to pray.

When faced with a battle between church members, step out of the center ring and drop to your knees. Appeal to God to bring clear vision and forgiving hearts together. You can't do it, but he most certainly can. I've seen it happen!

I love a happy ending, Lord! I need you to keep me in line. I need your Holy Spirit to remind me it's not my place to bring healing.

I can only imagine how it must hurt you to see your children fighting. Forgive me for getting ahead of you. Please help me to trust the prompting of your spirit and the teaching of your precepts.

Please protect me from the position of feeling like I need to choose sides. Give me boldness to speak the truth and good judgment to be the one who brings your love to the table. I don't ever want to be a part of dissension.

Make me a vessel of your peace!

Sweet bites of wisdom: Are you walking in unknown territory? If so, though you may not see anyone else there, you are not alone. God is always with you. If you wait on him, he will show you the way in his time, and it will be so much better than you could ever imagine. Stay in the Manual. It is truth and will prepare you for the curves that life can sometimes throw you. **—Robin Warren**[29]

Pick up your fork: Colossians 3:12-17

Colossians 3:12-17

Paul wrote to the believers in Colossae. The Holy Spirit gave Paul the needed instructions to help the people know how to walk with Christ in a challenging world.

I love our passage for today. It is step by step instructions that apply to every day.

Verse 12 lists five ways we are to approach and respond to all people. How will responding to the feuding in these ways help you remain neutral?

Verses 13-14 tell us of forgiveness and love. In most circumstances, this is what is needed to repair a broken relationship. Forgiveness and love.

Ever wish God would speak out loud and tell you what to do? Verses 15-17. These verses speak loud and clear. What is the Messiah's peace to control? What is the message of the Messiah to do among us? How are we to teach and admonish one another? And do everything in the name of ______ place your name here? No, the name of the Lord.

Weigh your words carefully when listening to disgruntled people talk about their frustration. Ask God to teach you to apply Colossians 3 and walk in it.

Chapter 24

Is It Well with My Soul? Remembering God is Faithful

Finding God in Your Faith Crises

> Have I not commanded you? Be strong and courageous! Do not tremble or be dismayed, for the Lord your God is with you wherever you go. (Joshua 1:9)

The notes to "It Is Well with My Soul" hung in the air, and I stood with the rest of the people and began to sing. That's what you do when you're in church, and everyone around you is singing.

You sing.

"When peace, like a river, attendeth my way, when sorrows like sea billows roll …"

Such a beautiful song.

"Whatever my lot, thou hast taught me to say. It is well, it is well with my soul."

But Lord … it is not well.

"It is well with my soul. It is well, it is well with my soul.[30]"

It is not well, Lord. And I don't think it can ever be well again.

I quit singing. I stood there, trying to quiet my thoughts and focus on the power, might, and love of the One for whom the song was written. I listened to the people around me as they sang. I briefly wondered if anyone was looking over at me … the preacher's wife who should be singing.

I did not sing another word that day. Instead, I quietly told God how afraid … no, desperate I was. I recalled to him all that had happened, and I reminded him that I was small up against this mountain.

As I begged him to miraculously fix what was broken, I remembered the clichés I had heard over the years:

"The God of the mountain is still God in the valley."

"If God brought you to it, he will bring you through it."

"Don't tell God how big the storm is, tell the storm how big your God is."

And I held to Scripture passages that over the years had become my best friends: John 14, Psalm 119, and Matthew 6.

I just don't feel it, Lord. you have the power, please just fix this. Just fix it. Then it will be well.

But you know, months turned into years before God's work—that was taking place all along—became evident. Oh, there were moments when I thought I saw a glimpse of sunrise. And there were days when I knew the sun had to be shining just above the angry clouds. God himself was the only One who knew my thoughts and the tossing and turning going on in my distressed heart.

Satan tried to tell me I was alone in the fight, that no person understood or cared. He tried to tell me God was off somewhere else in the universe, working in the lives of others ... you know, the ones who deserved his care.

I knew it then, and I know it today. God was always, always holding me. I may have struggled in his embrace as I tried to understand or change reality, but my battling didn't break his grip on my soul.

The strength of my faith doesn't change the power of my God.

Is it you?

Are you the one?

Are you the one this is for?

Could you be that person who has no name and yet, you are heavy on my heart? It is in the most difficult of days that we learn the most about God.

God is not Superman, a good luck charm, a deep-pocket grandfather, or multiple-choice buffet.

God is holy, all-knowing, loving, patient, kind and just.

GOD IS FAITHFUL.

He is always working in the lives of his kids.

On the longest and darkest of paths that we would never choose to walk is where God's character is revealed.

Perhaps you're tired of hurting. Maybe, today, you can't see the possibility of a ray of light. The strength of your faith doesn't change the power of God.

Keep asking.

Keep searching.

Keep knocking.

For in Jesus's own words "The one who asks receives, the one who seeks finds, to the one who knocks the door will be opened."

There's a verse in the song we seldom sing. Sing it as a prayer:

> *"But, Lord, 'tis for Thee, for Thy coming we wait, The sky, not the grave, is our goal; Oh, trump of the angel! Oh, the voice of the Lord! Blessed hope, blessed rest of my soul!"*

Sweet bites of wisdom: God is still here. He's still working. He's still planting ... still harvesting. Still pruning ... still blooming. Still plowing up the soil ... still designing landscapes of abundant fruit in our lives—a display of his splendor and nourishment for others. **—Joy Waters Martin**[31]

Pick up your fork: Isaiah 40:28-31

Isaiah 40:28-31

It's no surprise to God when we experience a season when it is not well with our souls. God never commanded us to understand him. He did, however, command us to trust him. In times of heartache or discontent, it's important to remind ourselves of his might and faithfulness. Read the passage in Isaiah 40.

Write a praise prayer, using these verses. Verbalize what is not well with you, then make a choice to trust God.

He is all you need.

Saving the Best Slice for the End of the Day: Remembering Who You Are and Whose You Are.

I married into a godly family. My sweet father and mother-in-law were examples of the goodness of Jesus from the very moment I first met them. They set a standard for living for their children and their children's children and their children's children's children! What a rich blessing they are!

My husband grew up with these words ringing in his ears any time he left the house: "Remember who you and whose you are, son."

Who is he? Well, he is a Pierce. He carries his father's name. His actions are a reflection of his father and mother.

Whose is he? He is a child of God. Because he belongs to the King, his life should be a picture of godly living.

Not only have we continued the tradition in telling our children to remember who they are and whose they are, my husband often tells the church family the same.

How about you?

When you put your feet on the floor this morning, did you remember who you are—you are the wife of a pastor, and whose you are—you are a child of the King?

What an honor!

Pumpkin Cookies

1 cup white sugar
1 cup canned pumpkin
1/2 cup softened butter
2 cups all-purpose flour
1 teaspoon baking soda
1 teaspoon baking powder
1 teaspoon cinnamon
1/4 teaspoon salt

Cream together butter and sugar until fluffy.
Add pumpkin and mix.
Sift together dry ingredients and fold into first mixture.

Drop by rounded tablespoonsful 2 inches apart on a baking sheet. Bake at 350° 10-12 minutes. Allow to cool before icing.

Icing:
1 cup confectioners' sugar
1 tablespoon softened butter
1/2 teaspoon vanilla extract
Small amount of milk (this is up to you and how thick or thin you like your icing)

Chapter 25

Shouldn't You Know How to Play the Piano?

Breaking the mold. Being who God created you to be.

> For we are His workmanship, created in Christ Jesus for good works, which God prepared beforehand so that we would walk in them. (Ephesians 2:10)

It's a running joke in churches all across America. The preacher preaches, and his wife plays the piano or the organ, right? I've been asked my fair share of times if I played. On the flipside, visitors almost always assume the lady playing the organ is the preacher's wife.

I tried to learn to play. Really I did. Sweet Mrs. Kibler met with me once a week for several years. She had taught countless children to play beautiful pieces and earn trophies galore. She threatened to hang them up from a sour apple tree when they didn't practice. Well, okay, yes … she threatened me as well. She was a dear senior adult friend in our church family who played the piano until her eyes failed her. And she gave it her best shot. The piano just wasn't for me.

But, children's ministries and Vacation Bible Schools, Sunday School and summer camps … now that was very much for me! God began his work in me when I was just a child. I can trace his footsteps and handiwork, molding me and teaching me, preparing me to work with children.

When our last child flew the coop, I experienced a minor midlife crisis. Who am I, really? Is this all there is? Should I go back to school? What does God want me to do?

I was lost for many months, quietly searching for God's next for me. I continued the work of ministry for preschool and children's families. All the while, wondering what God wanted of me and for me.

I suppose you can say he had writing in my future. He has opened doors and opportunities for this gift of words. I am excited and thrilled and thankful for what he is doing. How long will it last? I pray until the day I die! I pray I will always give him all the glory.

What are you thinking of as you read this devotion? Are you trying to force yourself into a manmade mold? Are you listening to your parishioners or have you asked God to show you his plan?

Are you learning to play the piano? Going to classes to perfect your writing skills? Studying your Bible, preparing for this Sunday's lesson for the ladies' class? Pulled out the sketch pad or dusted off your camera?

I have no doubt he has given you gifts. Gifts he wants you to use to bring others to him. Gifts to give him glory. Have you discovered them yet?

I assure you there is no greater joy than knowing God is using the gifts he gave you to make a difference in the lives of others.

I have a friend who is gifted with preschool children. They immediately love her and feel safe with her. She is using that gift to teach toddlers during the Sunday School hour. Those little people are learning of God's love from my friend. I suppose those who do not understand that gift would look in and say, "Isn't that sweet, she's playing with the kids." She and I know it might look like play to the untrained heart. In reality, she is leading little ones to love Jesus.

I think many of our churches are finally learning to step back and allow God to use us as he sees fit. For some, that means the piano is waiting. For others, there are classrooms full of children and adults who need teaching. Don't forget to look outside the church walls—crisis pregnancy centers, homeless shelters, and food banks. Maybe a community women's club is where he wants you to let your light shine. Have you discovered your God-giftedness?

Ask him to open your eyes and show you his plan for you. There is no joy like the joy of using your gifts to bring others to him. You don't have to fit in someone else's plan. You belong in the will of God alone!

It's me again, Lord. I'm searching for your plan for me. Please forgive me for choosing on my own. I'm sorry I run ahead of you.

Open my eyes and show me your will. I need faith and strength to follow, no matter where you send me. Help me to trust you fully and obey entirely.

Please place in my heart a longing for your plan for this season in my life. I know you will provide whatever is needed. I know you have already prepared me for this next step.

I love you, Lord! I love you and am so very thankful for your faithfulness in my life!

Sweet bites of wisdom: I sat beside my husband for the fifth time at the fifth church, with a search committee surrounding us, watching our every move and asking questions to learn our hearts and theology.

I had left the four previous interviews very discouraged because I had to answer no to the only question I was asked which was, "Are you able to play the piano or sing?" Satan had used the past interviews to feed lies into my head, leaving me feeling as if I just did not have the talents to be a pastor's wife or to fit the mold for what is required.

My husband answered his last question, and the head of the committee turned to me. I felt my palms get instantly warm and sweaty. But their question came as a refreshing wave, "What do you consider to be your spiritual gifts?" I felt a sense of relief and encouragement, as I realized I had been asked the right question!

Thankfully, this church understood there is not a set mold for what type of person God can use as a ministry partner. God will take the person he molded us to be and fit us perfectly into the body of Christ where he has called us to serve. **—Marcy Martin**[32]

Pick up your fork: 2 Timothy 1:8-12

2 Timothy 1:8-12

I read this letter to Timothy as if Paul is being young Timothy's cheerleader. It's full of encouragement and the message of "You can do it!"

Paul begins with thanksgiving and ends by telling Timothy not to quit until his mission is accomplished.

That's a great message for you and me. We have work to do. So, what exactly is it God wants us to do?

Meditate on verses 8-12 of chapter 1.

Write out your testimony. It's the beginning of your purpose.

Paul tells us in verse 11 what his purpose in Christ was. What has God set aside for you? If you are unsure, let me encourage you. Memorize the last part of verse 12. Ask God to show you his plan and then trust him to come through.

I've never believed God plays games with us. When we truly seek him and ask, he promised to answer.

What's next for you? God knows.

Chapter 26

Who Am I: Losing Track of Your Purpose

When you are busy living up to the expectations of others, you forget the only One who really matters.

> But seek first His kingdom and His righteousness, and all these things will be added to you. (Matthew 6:33)

Several years ago, Disney released a cute movie for kids about a fish that lost her way. Dory often reminded herself just to keep swimming. "Swimming, swimming, just keep swimming."

When our fourth child entered college, I found myself swimming. My heart for children's ministries was still passionate, but there was a place of emptiness ... an area of searching. I wondered if there was more. You know the answer to my questions, because you are reading this book. God gave me the desire of my heart to write and have the words read.

I don't know about you, but I want more from life than to "just keep swimming." Unless, of course, that's what God called me to do. But as I read my Bible and study the lives of his people, I have not yet found a person who was called just to keep swimming.

Perhaps we can change the wording a bit. How about "Trusting, trusting, just keep trusting." Sounds easy enough, right?

Or how about "Praying, praying, just keep praying"?

We can take a quick walk through the Old Testament and see what God had to say.

Adam and Eve: Obeying, obeying, just keep obeying.

Noah: Building, building, just keep building.

Abraham and Sarah: Believing, believing, just keep believing.

Jacob: Submitting, submitting, just keep submitting.

Joseph: Abiding, abiding, just continue to abide in me.

Moses: Relying, relying, just rely on me.

I think you get the picture. I invite you to continue the walk on your own. We have so much to learn from God's work in the Old Testament.

Where are you today? Do you find yourself swallowed up in the demands of your church people? This one thinks you should head up the women's ministry, that one believes missions is your calling, another demands your attention in the kitchen for fellowship meals. And here you are, rushing around trying to keep them all happy while at the same time keeping your home humming along and most likely going to work as well.

Gracious! Stop it! God didn't intend for you just to keep swimming!

Step back. For real. Tell your people you love them, but you are taking a break to be able to clearly hear from God. Vance Havner once said, "If you don't come apart, you will come apart!"

God has a specific plan for you. He's been using everything in your life to get you ready for the next assignment. It's exciting to spend some time looking back at his faithfulness in our lives. Don't skip it! Take time to write it down! Share it with your husband and with your kids. Share it with your friends! The Lord God is faithful from dawn to dusk and throughout the night!

Do you wish I could give you a step by step formula to know God's will for you? You know, one that only takes thirty minutes and the revelation is clear?

God doesn't work that way, and I am so glad. He wants to hear from you. He wants you to sit down and breathe him in. Be quiet. Listen. He will pour his faithful love all over you. And when the time is right, he will make clear what he has planned for you.

Looking back at the very beginning of my life in ministry with my forever partner, I would have been terrified had God shown me what he had in store for me thirty years down the line. I'm thankful, in his tender love and wisdom, he brought me along with baby steps. I'm grateful for his patience and forgiveness along the way.

I don't know what he has next for me. But that's okay, I can trust him no matter what my future holds.

Dory eventually finds her way. When she stops swimming in circles and follows the lead of one who knows better … how about you? Are you tired of swimming in circles?

Stop swimming, swimming and begin trusting, trusting.

> *To the Great Designer of all that is! I find myself trying to keep up with what people expect of me. I'm getting too tired. I'm empty. I'm wondering if this is all there is.*
>
> *Forgive me for losing sight of you. Forgive me for looking to others to find my way.*
>
> *I am ready, Lord, eager to hear what you have next for me! Well, I think I'm ready! I trust you to show me, in your good time, what is next for me.*
>
> *Until then, please quiet me. Lead me. Speak to me. Help me to stop talking and doing and start listening.*
>
> *Speak, Lord, I'm listening!*

Sweet bites of wisdom: As a young woman, I was observing and learning from our leader as she led with expertise the discussion in the women's small group. My thoughts wandered, and at that moment God planted a seed of possibility within my spirit. The seed was that one day in my future, I would lead a women's ministry that extended beyond the borders of my local church. I would bring women together, and the ministry would be inclusive of different denominational streams.

I was flabbergasted by the enormity of the possibility and dwarfed by my absolute lack of ability to bring it to pass even if I wanted to, which I wasn't exactly sure at that time that I did! I gave the whole idea back to God accompanied with a 'This is entirely beyond me, but it isn't beyond You. Let it be to me according to Your word.'

Time passed. I was asked to lead my own church's women's ministry where I personally grew, gained experience and developed my skill levels. All the while my love for and belief in God's outstanding design for women flourished. **—Di Finkelde**[33]

Pick up your fork: Read 2 Timothy 1:6-10 and 1 Corinthians 12:4-27

2 Timothy 1:6-10

God's will for all believers is sanctification—growing to be more like Jesus today than we were yesterday. Paul tells Timothy to fan into flame (stir it up) the gift God has placed inside us. The Holy Spirit was gifted to you and me the moment we invited Jesus to clean up our sinful hearts and live in us forever. Stir up your faith so it permeates every area of life.

Paul goes on to encourage Timothy to be bold and unashamed. It's interesting to me, Paul doesn't tell Timothy it's an easy ride. But he reminds Timothy of God's faithfulness.

This passage draws a picture for me. Imagine if you will, building a campfire that lights easily and warms you immediately. Time passes and you walk away from the blaze—maybe distraction nearby or preoccupation with your own thoughts. You feel a chill and remember the warmth of the fire. You return to find smoldering embers. It's still there, but no longer blazing.

The Holy Spirit will never leave you, but you cannot neglect him either. We fan the flame through personal prayer and daily devotion to scripture. We stir it up by walking the talk and acting on the truths he gives us.

What is your plan for stirring it up? If you don't have a plan, today is your day. Those who fail to plan, plan to fail.

Write your plan here.

____

____

____

____

1 Corinthians 12:4-12

As you "stir up" the Holy Spirit and he permeates every part of life, your unique purpose and giftedness will come into view. He will give you a longing, a desire, a love, a passion, a drive for what he has planned for you.

Read this passage in multiple translations. Pray your way through it and ask God to begin to reveal his will for you today.

What brings a strong response from you? List what matters most to you, as well as what you enjoy.

Brainstorm with God. How can these passions and talents be used to honor and glorify God? How do you plan to give your talents to God in order to grow the Kingdom?

Chapter 27

These Boots Were Made for Walkin'

Your congregation doesn't walk in your shoes, and it's okay.

> Therefore as you have received Christ Jesus the Lord, so walk in Him. (Colossians 2:6)

"Some people spend an entire lifetime wondering if they made a difference in the world. But, the Marines don't have that problem." Ronald Reagan made this comment on the occasion of the Marine Corps Birthday in 1985. The Marines indeed are an elite bunch. Their job is big, and their numbers are comparatively small.

You and I have a few things in common with them, but there's no need to tell them about it! This crazy, beautiful, trying, unusual, and amazing club we are in is really entirely exclusive. It's not for the weak or faint of heart.

I have joked with a few of my friends when they give me advice on things I should say, like "Tell them to mind their own business! You can have purple hair if you want to!" My response? "Honey, this is one reason God has not called you to be a preacher's wife!" We laugh about it and go our way. You and I know telling our church family to "mind their own business" would not be a good thing. That type of comment would not bring honor to God no matter who we are.

These shoes we wear ... they may appear to the untrained eye as sensible flats or maybe running shoes. But they are combat boots. They are steel-toed and tough. They are made for battles no one else understands.

Our most important job in this war is one of prayer warrior for the man who stands in the gap for the people of the church. The weight he carries is enormous. God has given him a responsibility even you and I cannot understand. So we pray. And we pray some more. And we listen to his heart and give him a safe, soft spot to land when he cannot give another ounce of himself. We support him with our words and actions.

And we pray some more. That is frontline in spiritual warfare.

Our combat boots take us down the hall to the bedrooms where our children sleep. We pray for our children, because they too are on the frontlines, and they don't even know it.

My combat boots take me to places of light-hearted laughter. I see it as my place to make my husband smile and laugh at goofy things. Maybe it's my purple hair, or perhaps it's a "see you later" wink. I used to put cereal in his shoes when he had a convention or a revival to preach, and I could not go with him. It was just another way to say, "Yup, I'm thinking of you!"

There are a few sweet ladies in my church who grew up as PKs. Every now and then, they come to me and tell me they are praying for me. They recount stories of their momma's life as the pastor's wife. They have the inside scoop, and I love how God uses them to encourage me.

We need to remember; the average church attendee doesn't have the slightest idea of the responsibility that came along with our MRS degree. And that's okay. God gives grace as it is needed. His grace is never wasted.

He sent his grace when I said, "I do," and I was clueless as to what I had just done!

He sent his grace when we moved from the only church I knew to a new congregation, away from home and family, away from familiar surroundings.

He sent his grace when I was alone and lonely, wondering if this was all there is.

He sent his grace when I looked up and found the dearest of his people, sweet friends who dropped by and were like a refreshing drink of water for my soul.

He sent his grace when my spirit was crushed by folks I dearly loved when they turned their backs to me and walked away.

He sent his grace when I found my place in his family, my gifts to use to honor him and bring others to him.

I don't know what tomorrow holds for me, but I do know he will send his grace for whatever he has planned.

These boots. They fit just right. They are a bit tattered by the miles they've walked. They are covered by his grace. They are ready for the next assignment.

> *Oh, Father! Thank you for your grace! I praise you for taking gentle care of my family and me. I adore you for my husband and for your attentive care for him!*
>
> *Please forgive me when I lose sight of your grace in my life. Help me to trust in your plan. Help me to be content knowing you understand and no one else needs to.*
>
> *Thank you for the people you place in my life, who say my name in prayer. It is humbling to know you love me that much!*
>
> *Make me an instrument of your peace today. Use me to show your love to a tired husband, to our kids who didn't ask for this role in their lives, and to the people I will meet today who are searching for you.*

Sweet bites of wisdom: Be YOURSELF. God created you TO BE YOU for a reason. Don't try to fit inside the box of expectation. Instead, use that thing that God has uniquely given to you. Someone needs it. **—Tammy Webb**[34]

Pick up your fork: Ephesians 5:1-20

Ephesians 5:1-20

Watching our granddaughter take her first steps was an exciting moment. Her first steps were wobbly. We cleared the way, making sure there were no toys to trip over or furniture to fall on. Each day she became a bit surer of herself, and soon, she was running around sure-footed.

Our walk with Christ might be compared to the first steps of a toddler. We begin our prayer life, Bible studies, and witnessing with a lot of trepidation over all that we do not know. If we persevere, we will grow in our knowledge, and the Holy Spirit will give us what we need to walk with purpose.

Take a moment and reread Ephesians 5:1-20. If we are imitators of God, what should be missing from our lives? List them here.

If we are imitators of God, there are specific instructions for what should be a part of our daily lives. List them here.

Paul tells the believers at Ephesus to pay careful attention to how they live—what they allow to be a part of their lives—and the message is for us too.

How will you make the most of the time?

Chapter 28

To Dream the Possible Dream: Dusting Off the Gifts God Gave You

Using your unique gifts to the glory of God.

> Thanks be to God for His indescribable gift. (2 Corinthians 9:15)

When I was a little girl, my dream for adulthood was to marry and have a family. All I ever wanted to do was be a mom. At some point in middle school through high school, the dream of writing began to take hold. I always loved words and writing came naturally to me, even as an elementary student.

I transitioned from high school straight into married life. In fact, Tommy told me when we were dating that we would marry after I graduated. I secretly took my GED and tested out in the eleventh grade! While that brought some shock to Tommy (hee hee), we were married just two months after I turned eighteen.

What it also brought was fear. Several years later, when I began to think and pray earnestly over the idea of writing, I wondered if a GED and no college degree would disqualify me. I opened the door, and Satan waltzed in. He told me I was dumb. Too dumb to be considered an author.

So, the dream was put on hold. For years.

When our fourth child entered elementary school, my husband encouraged me to apply to write children's Sunday school curriculum for LifeWay childhood publications. I was super-blessed to write for LifeWay for almost ten years. I have kept in contact with several friends made through the experience.

Sisters, I don't know if God would have opened those doors sooner had I not listened to the voice of fear. But I do know he has continued his work in me in every season of life. It's exciting to see the gifts used and dreams fulfilled.

What are you dreaming of today? Are you busy wiping noses and picking up toys? Or perhaps you're in carline with drive-through hamburgers waiting so kids can scarf them down before soccer practice?

Because I know God, I know he has gifted you with the ability to dream. Ask him. I dare you. Ask him to show you what he has planned. To show you what he is putting together, even now.

He's using every single experience in your life to mold you and get you ready for the adventure. He promised he would! That heartache? The one you said no good could ever come of … yes, he's using it. The moments you laughed and felt joy swell inside your heart? Yes, he's using it.

You are reading this wondering what's next or you already know what he has told you to do. Either way, I shout "Woo-hoo!"

Isn't it wonderful to know you can talk to him in carline and as you wipe that nose for the gazillionth time? There's only one thing standing between you and the goal God set for you. Fear. Give it to him today and get a move on!

I'm so excited for you!

I remember, Lord. I remember how fear flooded me at the thought of putting these words "out there" for people to pick apart. And I remember the freedom in giving the fear to you.

I am so thankful you are the giver of dreams. You, Father, are the One who makes a way for me to take what you have given me and turn it around to bring you glory. Thank you.

May the words of my mouth and the meditations of my heart forever and ever be pleasing to you and you alone!

Sweet bites of wisdom: *Arrgh! Someone just introduced me as "The Pastor's Wife" again. Did you see the expression change on that lady's face when the introductions were made?*

I often wonder if I would be perceived differently if I were simply introduced by my name. The first requirement of being a pastor's wife is to be a Christian. Therefore, I must pursue an understanding of my role as a "Christ follower." Romans 12:4-8 says that each Christian has particular gifts that contribute to the whole body. Take a peek at the varied expertise displayed by friends who are also in the pastorate.

Ginger excels in music.

Michelle has a burden for youth.

Claudia hungers to disciple the young married women in her congregation.

DeeAnn is a wizard with crafts and thrills others with her gifts.

Viva la Difference! If I tried to copy the talents given to these women, I would negate God's plan for *me*! I must therefore pursue my own identity. **—Sally Ferguson**[35]

Pick up your fork: Romans 12:6-8 and James 1:5-12

Romans 12:6-8

What did you dream of when you were just a little girl? Dreams of being a pilot or doctor, or engineer or mom—there's no wrong answer. What dream did you hide in your heart as a teenager or newlywed? Have you revisited yesterday's dreams to ask God if he has a use for them today?

I wonder if Paul (Saul) had dreams as a boy of what adulthood held. Did he dream of being a leader? Of being courageous?

Paul reminds the Christ followers in Rome to hold to the gifts given by God. What a scary time it must have been for them.

Are you able to place your fear where it belongs and ask God to reveal your gift and how he wants to use you?

James 1:5-12

Turn to James 1:5-12. You don't have to fear any part of your future. If you lack wisdom, what are you to do about it?

And what will God do? What is missing from God's answer?

There's no reproach. God doesn't criticize. We are safe asking for wisdom.

Maybe someday we will meet as we walk this broken world and you can tell me all about your journey and God's work. If not, we'll worship together where we will receive the crown of life and place all at his feet.

CHAPTER 29

The Desperate Call: Help! I'm on Hold!

What happens when you call a pastor's family hotline,
and they put you on hold?
It could happen!

> Be anxious for nothing, but in everything by prayer and supplication with thanksgiving let your requests be made known to God. And the peace of God, which surpasses all comprehension, will guard your hearts and your minds in Christ Jesus. (Philippians 4:67)

I had cried all morning. I was at a loss. There were no words. No sign of help. All I could do was cry.

And then I remembered hearing about a particular phone number for families in ministry.

That's it! I'll call and pour my heart out, and they will pray for me, and I will get through this!

So, I dialed this particular number.

"Hello, this is so and so with such and such ministries. How may I pray for you?"

And I began to cry again. I spit out a few words, choking on each one.

And it happened.

She said, "Ma'am, can you hold?"

I didn't say yes—she didn't allow me time to say anything. In a millisecond's time, the call went from "How may I pray for you?" to sending the soothing sound of an instrumental hymn.

Wow! Did that really just happen?

I sat there for a moment, stunned. At first, it felt like a slap in the face. But very soon after, I began to laugh. It wasn't the crazy kind of I-am-losing-my-mind kind of laugh. No. It was more like the why-haven't-I-taken-my-need-to-God-myself kind of laugh.

I hung up the phone and prayed. I poured my heart to God. And when I ran out of words, I knew he was still listening. He was listening to my heart. He wrapped his holy arms around me and whispered quietly, "Trust Me."

There is a kind of peace only the child of God knows. It is the peace he gives when we settle down and trust him.

I believe God uses hotlines and counselors and many organizations to help those of us who need "God with skin on" as we learn to trust him. I have sat on a counselor's couch numerous times, and I am so very thankful for people with that gift.

What I learned that day, I'm ashamed to say, I continue to learn.

Don't take the burden or worry to people before taking it to the Lord.

When something good happens, my first thought is to call my momma! When something bad happens, my first thought is to call my momma! As I write this chapter, my momma is in end-stage lung cancer and will soon be in the very presence of Jesus. Even though I know the time is here, I cannot imagine not having her to call.

But I have my heavenly Father to call on and say, "Look! Look what you did for me, Lord! I'm so excited for this new adventure! I'm thrilled to have this answer to my prayer!"

And I can call out to him and say, "Oh, dear God, I am at a loss. My heart. My heart is breaking, and I have no direction. I don't know what to do or say. I can't fix it. Please help me, Lord. Please. Help me."

He answers and says, "Come unto me all who are weary and heavy laden, and I will give you rest." (Matthew 11:28)

He reminds me, don't worry about these things. Instead, pray. And in exchange, he will send his peace, the kind of peace that surpasses any thought of peace I can possibly have. And his peace will guard my heart! (Philippians 4:6-7)

He's never put me on hold. He's never stepped away from me to give something else his attention. He has always stayed right by my side. Through victories and significant accomplishments, and through days and weeks of loss, his presence is real.

Where are you today? Are you in tears and at a loss? Are you celebrating great victories? God is right there. His presence is real. Call out to him!

I can't tell you I will never call another hotline again. Perhaps someday I will. I can say to you before I call anyone, I plan to call out to God. His presence is real.

> *You are the God of Abraham and Isaac. The God of Jacob. The God of Jesus! And you are my God! Please help me to think to talk with you first, whether I am on a mountaintop or trudging through a dark hour. I want to reach for you first.*
>
> *Thank you for providing people who love you and are here to point me back to you. Thank you for the many ways you meet my every need!*
>
> *I want to honor you on good days and on the days I struggle. I want to trust you to use everything in my life to drive me closer to you.*
>
> *Thank you for never putting me on hold. May I never take advantage of your patient love and provision that knows no boundary! I love you, Lord! I love you!*

Sweet bites of wisdom: But God never quits being patient with me. He is patient like the dishes in my sink. Like the laundry in my baskets. He is patient like that book that is still in my brain. Only with his unending patience comes compassion, understanding, and great love. He has shown me again and again through these decades marked by my imperfection that his grace never stops covering me. He is good. And his goodness keeps binding my wandering heart to my Savior. ~ **Melissa Edgington**[36]

Pick up your fork: 1 Peter 5:6-7 and Isaiah 53:1-12

1 Peter 5:6-7

You've heard before.

You've probably said it.

We grow when we go through hardship. Difficulties in life refine us and drive us to God.

The moment you near "the other side" of heartache, you know the saying is true.

When I read 1 Peter 5:6-7, I am reminded of Herbie the Dentist when he said, "What do you say we be independent together?" How often has that very statement been unspoken in my prayers?

It is humbling to admit I need help. What instructions does Peter give in verse 6?

There is security under the mighty hand of God, but we must humble ourselves to find it.

The word for "cast" used in verse 7 is also used in Luke 19:35 when the disciples "cast" their garments on the donkey for Jesus to ride into the city. Cast is exactly how it sounds, take it off of yourself and put it on something/someone else. God give us the written order to "cast off" our cares and anxieties by letting him bear them.

Write verse 7 in your own words. What are the cares and anxieties you need to cast on him? Is believing he cares for you enough for you to be able to *truly* give them to God?

Isaiah 53:1-12

We lost our first two babies to miscarriage. My heartache was unbearable at times. As I moved slowly though the grieving process, my anger and disappointment with God began to grow.

The Isaiah 53 passage was what the Holy Spirit used to begin healing my wounds and removing the bitter root. "And by his stripes, we are healed" opened my eyes to the suffering and love of Christ.

The very thought that his death on the cross and resurrection to new life not only brought the forgiveness of my sins, but also covered my pain. There is freedom in this truth!

Since those difficult months so many years ago, my husband and I have walked through deep and muddy waters. Holding to the Truth has never made the pain go away or the depression leave forever, but it has brought the promise of peace. The kind of peace unlike any other. The peace that says, "I am your God and will never leave you."

Study verses 1-12 of Isaiah 53. Pray over it. Search this passage for God's message for you today. Whatever you are going through, by his stripes you are healed!

Grandma Nellie's Peach Cobbler

1 stick butter

3/4 cup self-rising flour

3/4 cups white sugar

1/2 cup milk

1 can sliced peaches in heavy syrup

Mix together melted butter, sugar, flour, and milk until creamy
Pour into prepared 8x8 or loaf pan.
Pour peaches and syrup over the top. Do not mix.
Bake 350° for 25 minutes or until golden brown

Chapter 30

Lord, I Believe! Help My Unbelief!

When you reach a faith crisis.

> Now faith is the assurance of things hoped for, the conviction of things not seen. (Hebrews 11:1)

She buried her face in her hands and wept. She swallowed hard as if she could keep her grief from escaping. She spoke. The sentence was broken as she struggled to say each word, "I ... don't ... understand."

He sat in stillness. A single tear rested on his jawline. He stared at nothing as if it were something. Then came the long, heavy-shouldered sigh. *Maybe if I look long enough, I will understand.*

Am I guessing you've been there? Maybe you're there now. Each step you take to try to understand your painful situation or the condition of someone you love only leads you further away. Understanding isn't even a blip on the radar.

You feel the longing to understand and the greater hunger to believe God when he says "Trust Me."

We look to our spiritual leaders, those folks we think walk on mountaintops every day and we wonder how their faith grew to be so strong. *Do they ever question? Do they ever want to understand?*

We realize, to our church family, we are a spiritual leader. When we find ourselves questioning, we wonder if we are failing.

Questioning brings me to the passage telling us of the father who brought his son to Jesus (Mark 9). His son was troubled by a spirit that made him unable to speak. It would often throw the boy into fire or water.

I can't begin to relate to this father's anguish. To his sleepless nights and worry filled days.

He had done what he knew to do. He brought the boy to the disciples, and the disciples were unable to heal him. The father told Jesus his son had been this way since early childhood. I can hear his voice. The guttural groan of saying the words out loud. The deep ache of hearing his own words give testimony to how long his son had suffered. And how long, as the dad who could not fix it, he had anguished. And he did not understand.

Neither did he understand who Jesus was. When he spoke, he said, "Jesus, if you CAN." Jesus responded by saying everything is possible to the one who believes.

I can see it unfold as the father instantly cries out, "I believe!" but immediately realizes his faith is weak. It had been weakened by every healer or doctor or priest who may have been confident in helping the boy, and yet they failed and walked away. I see him drop his head and quietly murmur, "Help my unbelief."

Jesus commanded the spirit to leave the boy. And it went. The Scripture doesn't tell us any more about the father. I imagine he fell to the earth in a crumpled heap of gratitude and relief.

You know, he still did not understand.

I'm a lot like that father. I want to understand the whys and why nots, the hows and whens. But just like that father, it's not for me to understand.

God never said "Understand me." He said, "Love me, obey me, serve me, listen to me, TRUST ME."

Whatever your burden may be today, whether it is a new weight, or you have been troubled for years, maybe you needed to hear "You don't have to understand."

Be encouraged by God's promises never to leave you. He promises to work in your life and the lives of those you love even when you don't see it. He is faithful. When your faith feels weakened by the disappointments around you, well, that's the perfect time to resolve to trust him.

You know those people you think walk on mountaintops? They, too, have their moments of "Lord I believe! Help my unbelief." We all do.

God is faithful.

You are kind, Father. You provide for my every need. You even allow for me to ask for help to believe.

I am sorry for the many times I question. For the many times I try to figure out the best plan to fix whatever is wrong.

Help me to remember, even though I am looked to by some as one who leads, I am a follower. I need to follow you. Please fill me with your presence.

When I reach those moments of confusion, please, Father, help my unbelief.

I love You!

Sweet bites of wisdom: You might not see the light when your suffering is darkest, but God sees your tossing and your tears, and he is for you. You can trust him. You need not be afraid, though darkness be all around you, because God has delivered your soul from death and your feet from falling. You can even render thank offerings to him through the pain, because his promise is true. And even when no one else in this very public world knows your pain or your victory over it, he sees. He sees, he cares, he helps. And you may walk before him in the light of life that is abundant in spite of the pain. **—Monica Hall**[37]

Pick up your fork: Romans 5:1-5 and 1 Peter 1:6-7

Romans 5:1-5

I've been there. And so have you.

The darkness that creeps in and seems to envelope you. The whispered lies of hopelessness. And the loneliness that comes with it all.

Whether the crisis comes through your family, and you find yourselves in a place you never thought possible, or something terrible is taking shape on the church front—the desperation and pain are the same.

There was a time, in my younger years, when I believed in some unwritten protection from certain terrors of life. Protection that came along with serving in ministry. It wasn't that I thought we were special or different. I just assumed God provided a blanket covering certain things.

And then true life came my way. I began to learn sometimes the opposite is true. We've wrestled some demons *because* of our place in ministry.

Have you read Romans 5 lately? Paul—who knew tremendous suffering by the way—told the saints in Rome to rejoice in affliction. Using your own words, write out the reason he gave for our rejoicing.

Verse 5 reminds us of the source of our hope. Why does this hope not disappoint?

1 Peter 1:6-7

Genuine faith is valuable. What does Peter say is less valuable than proven faith?

If you often wonder why we must experience distress and trials, the answer is discovered in verse 7. Faith under pressure produces praise, glory, and honor for Jesus Christ.

Consider a recent trial. How have these three things manifested themselves through the pain?

We were never meant to figure it out or carry it alone. Jesus, who knows the pain of suffering, has promised to carry the load if we will just trust him with it. Will you give him the hopelessness you feel and ask him for light?

Chapter 31

Sit a Spell: Time at the Feet of Jesus

Keeping first things first.

> Rejoice always; pray without ceasing; in everything give thanks; for this is God's will for you in Christ Jesus. (1 Thessalonians 5:16-18)

I have a few friends who enjoy photography. My sister has had an eye for taking beautiful photographs since she was very young. We've gone picture happy now that we have cameras on our phones. Seems there is never a missed shot … the Facebook world is an excellent example of photo-crazy. We certainly could do without some of the pics we can never un-see …

When I talk about photography, I am referring to the kind that requires skill and that special something that allows the photographer to see what no one else sees just yet. These kinds of pictures are captured by an eye behind the camera that focuses on a specific subject in the frame. Along with skill and knowledge, the best shots are achieved through experience.

The headline of your previous week depends on your focus. Sometimes the people around you do not know your focus. You know how it is, folks say "Hey, how ya doin'?" and without a single thought you reply "Fine" "Good" "No complaints." And in your heart, you cry "I'm glad I'm standing" "I'm tired" "I don't think I can do this much longer."

As a believer in the power of God, it is both my duty and my choice to place my focus on my Savior instead of my surroundings, my Father and not my failures, my Provider and not my problem, his peace in place of my pain.

Over the years, Psalm 119 has become my personal retreat center. It is where I turn when I do not know where else to go. This chapter is the longest in the Bible, penned by David, and is rich in life-giving words of wisdom. This chapter gives me focus on life. It is where I often choose to sit a spell at the feet of Jesus.

After completing a lengthy study on Psalm 119, C.H. Spurgeon wrote: "Those who have never studied it may pronounce it commonplace, and complain of its repetitions; but to the thoughtful student it is like the great deep, full, so as never to be measured; and varied, so as never to weary the eye. Its depth is as great as its length; it is mystery, not set forth as mystery, but concealed beneath the simplest statements; may I say that it is experience allowed to prattle, to preach, to praise, and to pray like a child prophet in his own father's house?"[38]

David was no stranger to loss and pain. We like to remember and teach his victories—Goliath's defeat, David's conquest over tens of thousands, and the day he was chosen as God's man for the people. Woven throughout the victories of his life, are the greatest of sorrows. David experienced the disappointment of failure, the distress of running and hiding for his life, the deep despair in the death of a child, the rebellion of a son, and immense shame before God.

The overflow of God's grace in his life produced the words of Psalm 119. Walk with me a moment and view the focus of David's life:

> [1]How happy are those whose way is blameless,
> who live according to the LORD's instruction!
> [7]I will praise You with a sincere heart
> [16]I will delight in your statutes;
> I will not forget Your word.
> [25]My life is down in the dust;
> give me life through Your word.
> [37]Turn my eyes
> from looking at what is worthless;
> give me life in your ways
> [55]Yahweh, I remember your name in the night,
> and I obey Your instruction.
> [64]LORD, the earth is filled with your faithful love
> [108]LORD, please accept my willing offerings of praise
> [147]I rise before dawn and cry out for help;
> I put my hope in Your word.

> [165]Abundant peace belongs to those who love your instruction;
> [172]My tongue sings about Your promise, for all Your commands are righteous.

And my favorite verse in the chapter, the verse that is my anchor in every storm:

> [112]I am resolved to obey Your statutes to the very end. (Christian Standard Bible)

I am no Pollyanna. I will never try to get you to see the rainbow during the storm. I will encourage you to change your focus. No matter who you are—disappointment, confusion, and frustration are present in every frame. When you focus on those things, you will allow a perfect breeding ground for bitterness and compounded sorrow. Allow me to encourage you to look to the One who holds the world together. Sit at his feet and allow his love to envelop you.

Focus on his truth.

Focus on his sovereignty.

Focus on his faithfulness.

I have seen beautiful images where the eye of the photographer focused her camera on the most crucial subject in the frame. The blurring of the surroundings added to the depth of brilliance and importance of the primary focus.

I sincerely hope you know the Savior. I sincerely hope you are growing in your faith. As you choose to practice his precepts or, better put, resolve to obey his rules for life, you will find he is forever faithful to keep his promises. There is an anchor in life's storms.

Maybe your headline next week could read:

The Anchor Holds

God is Faithful

I Believe

I Am Resolved to Keep God's Statutes until the End.

Sweet bites of wisdom: Working for him should never crowd out worshipping him. Devotion always comes before duty." **~Heather Proctor**[39]

Pick up your fork: Isaiah 55

Isaiah 55

God speaks through Isaiah and invites you and me to run to him and live. Please notice, the invitation is for *everyone who thirsts*.

Are you thirsty? Do you hunger for more of God? If you find yourself content in your relationship, this invitation is no longer for you. Harsh words, I know. But not my words. God wants those who hunger and thirst for him to come, listen, and live.

There is only one option for the woman who isn't thirsty—repentance. A time of soul-baring confession. The kind where you ask forgiveness for what you know and ask God to reveal what you don't know. Self-sufficiency is a terrible sin to bear. I fight against it all the time. I often think I know what to do and how to do. It creeps in like a nasty fog. I don't see it coming until it envelops me.

Isaiah 55 is a beautiful passage to study at Jesus's feet. Scripture quenches thirst and at the same instant creates hunger.

As you read the chapter, jot down the verses that speak the loudest.

Be still.

Be quiet.

What is God communicating to you today?

How will you be different because of your time with him?

He is faithful!

Granny's Banana Bread

1 cup of white sugar

1 stick softened butter

2 eggs

3 ripe, mashed bananas

1 teaspoon baking soda

1/2 teaspoon baking powder

1-1/4 cup all-purpose flour

Cream together sugar and softened butter.

Add eggs and bananas.

Sift together dry ingredients and add to sugar mixture. Stir until combined.

Pour into prepared loaf pan. Bake 350° for 1 hour. Bread is done when a toothpick inserted in the center comes out clean.

Chapter 32

The Child of the King: Garments of White Awaiting

The Scriptures are clear—the crown of life is given to those who overcome. You can do it!

> He who overcomes will thus be clothed in white garments; and I will not erase his name from the book of life, and I will confess his name before My Father and before His angels. (Revelation 3:5)

She was short.
Her laughter filled the room.
She was bold.
She was opinionated.
She was passionate.
She loved Jesus.
And she battled cancer for more than twelve years.

Her name was Lisa, and I, along with countless others, loved her deeply. She was a loyal friend, unafraid to tell me when I was wrong and always standing nearby to cheer me on.

Lisa epitomized "overcoming." She was a Sunday school teacher, special education teacher, and Mom to two. She didn't allow cancer, procedures, treatments, or surgeries to rule her life. She looked at every new day as an opportunity to live. And live she did.

I would love to finish her story by saying overcoming meant she beat the dreaded "C" in a way that allowed her to remain here to see her kids into adulthood. She died too soon. Overcomer? Oh, yes! I love to think of what it was like that December day, as her family and friends wept over our loss. She stepped into God's presence and received her garment of white. Maybe she heard "Well done" or "You fought the good fight and finished your course."

I can hear it as Jesus made the announcement, "Father! This is Lisa! She is mine. She is a victor and walks worthy to be dressed in white!"

What kind of day are you experiencing? Is it one of those just-get-through-it annoying kind of days filled with lost keys, fighting kids, and burned cookies? Maybe it's a day that you can only describe as warfare. Or perhaps you are enjoying a day of sunshine and smiles.

I'm going to share with you some "overcomer" advice my friend Lisa often repeated to me. She would walk up to me, hand turned upward and closed tightly. Then she would slowly open her hand to palm up and say, "This is Shelley. Letting go."

Overcoming often begins with letting go. Letting go of bitterness. Letting go of failure. Letting go of misunderstanding.

Once we let go of those things, our vision clears, and we are able to be useful examples of Jesus to those around us, whether it is our sweet little preschool kids or our coworkers. We begin to overcome, day by day, without even being aware of the struggles.

I don't know what my future holds, but it's beautiful to know who holds it! I'm going to wear white one day, y'all! So will you!

I have these days, Lord, when I forget what's important. Some people make me so angry I could scream. Some days, I am tired before I even put my feet on the floor. And honestly, sometimes I don't want to overcome.

Forgive me, please, for losing sight of you. Forgive me for choosing defeat.

I want to walk worthily in life of wearing white when I see you. Please keep me ever mindful of what matters most. Please use my life to make others want what I have—you!

What great opportunities you lay before me! What a wonderful responsibility!

Keep me! Hold me! Use me!

Sweet bites of wisdom: There is no greater motivation for pursuing the one perfect relationship in your life than understanding how imperfect your human relationships are. For every disappointment you experience with a friend or congregant, for every word spoken behind your back, every misrepresentation or even outright lie about something you said or did, and every attempt to undermine your ministry for no other reason than it isn't exactly what one person thinks it should look like, God offers not only his grace, but his power and approval.

How earnestly does Paul remind us that God's power is made perfect in our weakness? (2 Corinthians 12:9) That by sharing in the sufferings of Christ, we are sharing also in the comfort only he can give? (2 Cor. 1:5)

Would we forfeit this for a few less struggles? Some days in our weakness, maybe so. But OH, what a paltry and temporary reward that would bring.

There is not a single moment of your ministry over which God is not sovereign. Which of course, doesn't mean it will be easy. Let's not forget Isaiah 6. But if God has called you, he will not abandon you. Nor will he be surprised by the difficulties you face along the way. He is with you. Always with you.

For whatever reason, I felt like someone might need to read that today. Read the warnings too. All of them. Most of them are painfully true. Prepare accordingly. Christian ministry is not an easy life and shouldn't be entered lightly. But nor should it be feared. We serve a mighty, mighty God whose sustaining power reigns over every hurtful relationship we will ever encounter. That doesn't mean we don't feel real pain. Sometimes enduring pain. It just means we get to feel real comfort and peace too. The kind that comes with power, and the kind that fills eternity. **—Becky Wilson**[40]

Pick up your fork: Philippians 1:1-11

Philippians 1:1-11

My first Bible was a gift for my fifteenth birthday, given to me by my mom and dad. My mom, in her beautiful script handwriting, inscribed the reference Philippians 1:6. I'm thankful for the vivid memories of that special day.

I was a baby believer then, hungry and thirsty to know more about Jesus. How much faith is needed to believe God will complete what he began? Do you believe he is working in you to complete what he started in you?

Journal about the day you asked Jesus to be your Savior, the day he began working in you. Whether that day was last year or thirty years ago, what evidence do you see of his hand in your life?

Are you thankful?

Are your prayers full of joy?

Is your knowledge growing?

Are you telling others they can experience the peace you know?

As out love grows in knowledge and discernment, God weaves his grace throughout each experience in life. One day, we will stand, filled with the fruit of righteousness, before Jesus. He will tell the Father we are his.

We'll wear white.

Chapter 33

Build Your House on the Lord Jesus Christ.

Get the foundation right.

> Therefore thus says the Lord God, Behold, I am laying in Zion a stone, a tested stone, A costly cornerstone for the foundation, firmly placed. He who believes in it will not be disturbed. (Isaiah 28:16)

Tommy and I married in November 1981. I like to look back at the years that often feel like they took minutes to pass.

Our first years together were not a cakewalk. We had a lot of adjusting to do. Tommy had lived on his own for several years, and I had never lived anywhere but in my parent's home. He preferred hospital corners when making a bed. I … well, I didn't know what a hospital corner was!

I cried a lot and didn't even know why.

He was in seminary, and I hardly saw him. Hmm, perhaps that is why I cried!

We were broker than broke those first few years, but we didn't mind eating boxed mac and cheese and playing Yahtzee on date night.

We suffered the loss of two babies. Oh, how we grieved.

Our first move came and the birth of our first child shortly afterward. It was the first time I lived "long distance" from my mom. Some of you remember way back in pre-cell phone days when you had to count every penny, and phone calls weren't free.

Our next move was even farther from my mom. Our first home, purchased in Northern Kentucky, where we welcomed two more children.

I was too busy caring for the babies to cry.

Tommy was still gone all the time. The pressures at this church were great.

Our last move came four years later. We landed in Greeneville, Tennessee, where our last baby was born.

When we walked through the door of Towering Oaks the first time, we knew we were home.

Home.

Home. What a wonderful word.

The next twenty-eight plus years have been full. Full of:

Laughter
Trial
Growth
Friendship
Betrayal
Joy
Pride
Sorrow
Confusion
Cheering
Success
Failure
Crying
Talking
Breathing
And a lot of praying.

We are now grandparents and my, oh my, oh my, oh my, what fun!

I have some advice for the newly married, barely married, hardly married, and happily married.

Build your home on the Lord Jesus Christ. The parable of the foolish and wise men is a clear picture of the difference in trusting God for all your needs and leaning on your own understanding.

Being married is tough work. Being married in ministry is even tougher. Neither Tommy nor I are the same people we were in 1981. We "suffered" through our growing pangs and chose to grow closer together in them. We held to the promises we made to each other and to the promises of God. The most significant and best hope is the faithfulness of God. He is truly faithful. Had we tried to do this life on our own we would never have made it.

Our son is building a playhouse in the backyard for the nieces and nephews. He took great care with its foundation. He wants a structure that will last and hold up under the assault of weather and children! Lilley looks out the window at it and says, "John did it."

I'm looking back at our years of marriage, and I'm saying "GOD DID IT! Wow, yes, God did it!"

> *Father, wasn't is just yesterday we said, "I do"? Time has a way of speeding past us. I like to look back at your faithfulness over the years. You have kept every promise. You have provided in every hour.*
>
> *Even as I pray today, you are making provision. I hear your faithfulness in the songs of birds. I see your faithfulness in the rising sun. I feel your faithfulness in the hugs of my grandchildren. Your faithfulness is everywhere.*
>
> *Help us, as we serve you, to be faithful until you call us home.*

Sweet bites of wisdom: Personally, I feel there is no higher calling, no greater task than this. In working towards excelling as the helpmeet God wants me to be to my pastor-husband, I am also liberated to fulfil the potentials of being a woman of God.

Today's woman is trying to stretch herself into a number of roles at the same time. She wants her own identity, she wants a career, she wants accomplishments to show, and so on. Many pastors' wives fall into this trap of activities. So, like a typical pastor's wife, I had my hand in more activities in the church than is really necessary.

Early one morning, the beginning of yet another hectic day, God spoke to me about my lifestyle. I was too busy for his liking. He reminded me that he is not a slave driver. I began to release one responsibility after another. I realized that I could be replaced in all my activities, responsibilities and roles in the church, but no one could fill my place as wife to my husband, Prince, or as mother to our children, Pammie and Jimmy. Now all my ministries in the church flow from being the helpmeet God intended me to be. I am still busy. I am still involved in the church, but whatever I do is the result of being the pastor's helpmeet. **—Petrina Guneratnam**[41]

Pick up your fork: Matthew 7:24-29, Matthew 5-7

Matthew 7:24-29

The wise man built his house upon the rock, house upon the rock, house upon the rock and the rains came tumbling down.

Such a fun little song we teach the kids. So fun, we easily overlook the heavy application.

How does Jesus describe the one who hears his words and acts upon them?

How does he describe the one who hears and does nothing?

Upon who does the rain fall?

When our newlywed daughter lamented her bills that began to pile up, my not-so-compassionate-reply was "#adulting."

Life's rain falls on the just and the unjust. Bills, illness, broken refrigerators, and flat tires are part of life on earth. Temptations to turn from God in bitterness or in search for something better will come along. Satan watches and waits for the right exhausted and heartbroken moment to call us to an "easier" existence.

Verse 24 begins with the word "therefore." Let's look at what the therefore is there for.

Matthew 5-7

Matthew chapters 5-7 are the words Jesus is referring to. These chapters are packed with truth for living. Truth that builds the strong foundation that holds up under life's rain.

The Sermon on the Mount is more like a Thanksgiving feast than a devotional snack. Take the time to savor these words. They belong to you and me!

Chapter 34

The Last Word: Be of Good Cheer

This gift of First Lady is a grand opportunity to serve God exceptionally. Embrace it and lean on God. He's all you need.

> These things I have spoken to you, so that in Me you may have peace. In the world you have tribulation, but take courage; I have overcome the world. (John 16:33)

There are milestones in life parents contemplate as their children grow. Driver's license, high school, college, and marriage come to mind. Sons and daughters, ready to take on the world, unaware of exactly what that means. We wait for the opportunity to have "that talk" with our kids. We remind them of all that we have taught them.

Blink your eyes, and you'll find your baby boy standing there, uncontrollable grin on his face, holding his brand-new license, asking the question we dread.

"Can I have the keys?"

"I don't know, can you?" responds the grammar police in your household.

Cue the talk.

"Wear your seatbelt. Don't drive over 45[mph]. Put your phone away. Pay attention and don't tailgate. Rolling stops are illegal. If you have the music too loud, you won't be able to hear emergency vehicles or trains. Let me know when you get there."

"Ma, I'm only going around the block."

Matthew 13-17 allows us the privilege of knowing Jesus's heart as he reminded his disciples all he had taught them over the previous three years.

He knew his last words would ring in their hearts in the coming days of uncertainty.

With all authority, Jesus instructed the disciples and all who would read his words for generations to come. These final words are for you and for me.

Follow my example of servanthood.
Love each other as I have loved you.
Don't worry; I'm coming back.
I am the Father.
Ask in my name.
Keep my commandments.
The Comforter will be with you.
Remain in me.
The world will hate you.
Life will be difficult.
I tell you these things so you will have peace.

Jesus knew his friends wouldn't understand what was about to happen. We know that Jesus would soon be arrested, beaten and crucified. We see the weight of these last words.

Jesus's words before his crucifixion are for us as well. Matthew 17 records how he prayed for himself, his disciples, and all believers.

I don't make light of the difficult seasons we experience merely because we have married into the ministry. We could all describe days of wishing we could curl up in a ball and make the world go away. We could also tell stories of precious people who lift us up in prayer and do what they can to lighten our load.

While it is true we wear a bulls-eye target in the realm of spiritual warfare, it is most important to remember we belong to the Prince of Glory.

We have a choice to make every day. We can choose to put our trust in our own abilities and our focus on the enemy or we can decide to put on the full armor and get on with our Father's business.

Precious First Lady, whether you have been the preacher's wife for decades and could have written this book, or you are brand new to this gig, this is for you. Don't be afraid to put on your ratty robe, grab an oversized cup of creamer with a bit of coffee, kick the toys on the family room floor to the side and take a seat. Remove the hats you wear and just be you—warts and all.

We are a team of special forces. A band of faithful women who can laugh together, cry together and get angry together. Most of all, we can trust God to be all we need as we recognize this incredible gift that he has given us—the opportunity to be a part of Kingdom work in a way that only a pastor's wife is able.

Let's do this!

I freely admit to you today—I cannot do this one. Single. Day. Without you. Help me, as I study your words, to clearly understand your plan, cautions, expectations, and promises.

Thank you for words that give me hope for a better today. Strength for a life that honors you. Power to live in a way that makes a difference.

Please forgive me when I forget your example and admonitions.

I love you, Lord. I want to honor you all of my days.

Sweet bites of wisdom: *The end of all things is near.* Do you hear the ticking of the clock? *Time's short. Jesus is coming.* To follow Christ is to live with expectation—anticipating the day Christ pulls back the veil of eternity and returns for his own. This world we see and touch will not endure forever. We are made for greater things. Eternal things. And so even as the sand of time pours away from beneath our feet, we plant ourselves on the solid ground of Christ and cling to the three things that are eternal: God. God's Word. And the souls of men and women. **—Leigh Powers**[42]

Pick up your fork: Psalm 119:65-80, Psalm 112.

Psalm 119:65-80

The focus of Psalm 119 is on gaining strength and joy in keeping God's precepts. How does the resolve to obey God's statutes give you the power to remain confident in God when ministry is smooth sailing as well as when conflict rises? List the ways he has proven himself faithful in your life.

As I have struggled with various difficulties in life—both personal and in ministry—God has provided for every need through the words in Psalm 119.

He is providing for you as well. Spiritual, physical, emotional, and mental strengthening is ours for the seeking and asking.

Choose a key verse from our 119 passage and commit it to memory. Recall it in sorrow and joy, in need and in completeness. Know that God loves you.

Free will. We have free will to choose Jesus and life or our own way and certain death. Our children and grandchildren have free will and choices to make. Every person who enters our churches and every face we see as we go our merry way have the gift of free will.

What makes the difference? How can we live a righteous life, smack in the middle of free will and difficult experiences? Is it possible to be like Jesus in our houses made of glass?

Psalm 112

Blessed is the man who …

Verse 7 is the key to righteousness. What does a "steadfast heart" mean?

If you are anxious because you feel the weight of watching eyes, take a moment to breathe. Notice God's instructions are not predicated by whom you are married to or how many ministries you find yourself leading. His precepts are the same for all believers. A steadfast heart is required of all of us. Trusting in the Lord is the foundation of faith.

What are you doing on purpose each day to strengthen your faith? To walk in righteousness? To act on what you believe?

It's Just Beginning …

Today is the first day of the rest of your life. The Bible puts it a far better way—his mercies are new every morning.

Wherever you are in your journey, my prayer for you is that you will know God's presence, peace, and guidance. That you will see his hand working in and through you to make a difference in this broken word.

I pray you will stand strong in his power alone under the weight of it all, knowing he will provide in the darkest hour.

May you see his grace at every turn, in the face of every child and the warmth of every sunrise. May you know that you know that you know he is faithful.

May you take the treasure he has given you and freely share it in your life. Be bold presenting the gospel, knowing Christ died once for all and lives today.

Most of the "Sweet bites of wisdom" quotes were taken from blogposts of women just like you and me. You'll find the blog addresses in the bibliography. I encourage you to check them out.

Don't be a lone wolf. Social media has offered a wonderful opportunity to connect with each other. Don't be afraid to reach out!

I'm proud of you. I'm thankful for you. In my heart of hearts, I love you!

Steady on!

No Bake Chocolate Peanut Butter Cookies

By Cyndi Pierce Vogt

2 cups white sugar

1/4 cup unsweetened cocoa

1 stick of butter

1/2 cup milk

1 teaspoon vanilla

3 cups quick oats

1/2 cup peanut butter

Mix sugar, cocoa, milk, and butter together over medium heat. Bring to a boil. Boil for 1 minute exactly.

Remove from heat and add oats, vanilla, and peanut butter.

Stir until combined and drop by rounded teaspoons onto buttered wax paper.

Endnotes

1. Janet Vines, received via email June 6, 2017, used with permission

2. June Bodenhamer, received via messaging August 25, 2017, used with permission

3. Annie Hawks. 1872. "I Need Thee Every Hour." Public Domain

4. Elizabeth Elliot, "40 Inspiring Quotes from Elisabeth Elliot," Debbie McDaniel, Crosswalk.com June 17, 2015 https://www.crosswalk.com/faith/spiritual-life/inspiring-quotes/40-inspiring-quotes-from-elisabeth-elliot.html September 24, 2018

5. Joyce Rogers, "Joyce Rogers imparts wisdom from her 48 years of marriage," Macon Fritsch, Baptist Press, October 14, 1999, http://www.bpnews.net/94 September 24, 2018

6. Anne Graham Lotz, "Ruth Bell Graham: The Life of a Mother," Billy Graham Evangelistic Association, May 12, 2017, https://billygraham.org/gallery/ruth-bell-graham-the-life-of-a-mother/ September 24, 2018

7. Ruth Bell Graham, "Marriage Encouragement from Ruth Bell Graham," Billy Graham Evangelistic Association, June 9, 2016, https://billygraham.org/story/marriage -encouragement-from-ruth-bell-graham/ September 24, 2018

8.Hilda Pierce, received in person November 28, 2017, used with permission

9. Jill Briscoe, "Reaching Women for Jesus," Just Between Us, Laurie Beyer, http://justbetweenus.org/ministry/ministry-life/inspiring-stories-of-christian-ministry/ September 24, 2018

10. Elisha Galotti, "Your Family Isn't Perfect and Neither Is Mine (Part 2)," True Women, September 17, 2014, https://www.reviveourhearts.com/true-woman/blog/your-family-isnt-perfect-and-neither-is-mine-part-/ September 24, 2018

11. Shonda Kuehl, "Who Does the Pastor's Wife Talk To?" The Nutty Pastor's Wife, March 4, 2014, https://thenuttypastorswife.wordpress.com/2014/03/08/who-does-the-pastors-wife-talk-to/ September 24, 2018

12. Thom Rainer, July, 18 2011, "When Pastor's Suffer Depression," https://thomrainer.com/2011/07/when pastors experience depression/ September 29, 2018

13. Mark Chanski, "Suffer From Depression? Spurgeon did too." May 4, 2012, https://markchanski.com/2012/05/04/suffer-from-depression-spurgeon-did-too/ September 29, 2018

14. Ryan Griffith, July 6, 2017, "Martin Luther's Shelter Amid the Flood of Depression," ww.thegospelcoalition.org/article/martin-luthers-shelter-amid-flood-of-depression/ September 29, 2018

15. Dr. Joel Beeke and Randall J. Pederson, Jonathon Edwards (1703-1758), Meet the Puritans,https://www.monergism.com/thethreshold/articles/onsite/meetthepuritans/jonathanedwards.html September 29, 2018

16. Heather Platt, "Heather Platt Interview, Part Two," Girltalk, May 31, 2012, http://www.girltalkhome.com/blog/heather-platt-interview-part-two/ September 24, 2018

17, Kay Warren, received via email November 8, 2017, used with permission

18. Mary Mohler, "Mary Mohler, The Interview Part 2," Girltalk, September 19, 2007, http://www.girltalkhome.com/blog/Mary_Mohler_The_Interview_Part_2/ September 24, 2018

19. Teri Brooks, "Pastor's Wives and Depression, Married to a Pastor, March 3, 2016, http://marriedtoapastor.com/depressed-pastors-wife/ September 24, 2018

20. Shirley Unrau, "The Honest Journey of a Pastor's Wife," The Life, https://thelife.com/the-honest-journey-of-a-pastors-wife September 24, 2018

21. Lori Wilhite, "Leading and Loving It: Pastors' Wives Overcome Depression," October 25, 2011, Gabrielle Devenish, The Christian Post, https://www.christianpost.com/news/leading-and-loving-it-pastors-wives-overcome-depression-59284/ September 24, 2018

22. Barbara Miller Juliani, "Thoughts on Being a Pastor's Wife," CCEF, June 28, 2017, https://www.ccef.org/resources/blog/thoughts-pastors-wife September 24, 2018

23. Christine Hoover, "Hello, I'm the Pastor's Wife," Grace Covers Me, June 20, 2013, http://www.gracecoversme.com/2013/06/hello-im-pastors-wife.html September 24, 2018

24. Jacki C. King, "To The Weary Pastor's Wife," SBC Voices, June 26, 2018, https://sbcvoices.com/to-the-weary-pastors-wife/ September 24, 2018

25. Debbie McDaniel, "8 Powerful Promises From God," Crosswalk.com, June 14, 2017, https://www.crosswalk.com/blogs/debbie-mcdaniel/ September 24, 2018

26. Martha Fry, "As A Pastor's Wife, How Do You Handle Friends In Church?" ARC, October 3, 2011, https://www.arcchurches.com/as-a-pastors-wife-how-do-you-handle-friends-in-church September 24, 2018

27. Shannon Parish, "The Role of a Pastor's Wife," Sarah's Tent, http://sarahstent.com/articles/role-of-pw.htm September 24, 2018

28. Whitney Hopler, "Pastor's Wives: Enjoy Your Lives," Crosswalk.com, February 24, 2005, https://www.crosswalk.com/church/pastors-or-leadership/pastors-wives-enjoy-your-lives-1314981.html September 24, 2018

29. Robin Warren, "Evil Instruction Booklets!" Conversations From My Laptop, Some Thoughts From a Pastor's Wife, April 9, 2015, http://thepastorswife.org/tag/thing-doer/ September 24, 2018

30. Horatio Spafford. 1873. "It Is Well With My Soul." Public Domain

31. Joy Waters Martin, "Stomping It Out With Jesus," A Life-giving Moment, April 28, 2018, https://alifegivingmoment.wordpress.com/2018/04/28/stomping-it-out-with-jesus September 24, 2018.

32. Marcy Martin, received via email May 4, 2018, used with permission

33. Di Finkelde, "How To Overcome The Reality Of Feeling Invisible," Conversations with a Pastor's Wife, August 22, 2018, http://www.conversationswithapastorswife.com/blog/ September 29, 2018

34. Tammy Webb, received via messaging August 9, 2018, used with permission

35. Sally Ferguson, "My Name is NOT The Pastor's Wife!" Just Between Us, https://justbetweenus.org/ministry/pastors-wives/my-name-is-not-pastors-wife/ September 24, 2018

36. Melissa Edgington, 41 Years Old, Your Mom Has A Blog, July 29, 2018, https://yourmomhasablog.com/2018/07/29/41-years-old/ September 24, 2018

37. Monica Hall, "Silent Suffering in an Instagram World," True Woman, December 14, 2017 https://www.reviveourhearts.com/true-woman/blog/silent-suffering-instagram-world/ September 24, 2018

38. C.H. Spurgeon, The Treasury of David, Funk & Wagnalls, 1888
vi

39. Heather Proctor, received via messaging September 3, 2018, used with permission

40. Becky Wilson, "Honored to be Dishonored," For The Church, February 3, 2016, https://ftc.co/resource-library/blog-entries/honored-to-be-dishonored September 24, 2018

41. Petrina Guneratnam, "The Pastor's Wife as a Helpmeet," Christian Assemblies International, https://www.cai.org/bible-studies/pastors-wife-helpmeet September 24, 2018

42. Leigh Powers, "Time's Short. Love Well," Leigh Powers, Finding My Place in God's Story, March 23, 2017, http://leighpowers.com/2017/03/23/times-short-love-well-1-peter-47-11/ September 24, 2018

About the Author

Shelley Pierce and her husband, James (AKA Tommy), live in the mountains of East Tennessee where he pastors Towering Oaks Baptist Church in the town of Greeneville. She serves alongside him on staff as Director of Preschool and Children's Ministries. Together they raised four children and now enjoy the gift of grandchildren.

Married into ministry over thirty-five years, Shelley has a passion for reaching out to what some refer to as "the loneliest women in the church," the pastors' wives. She has experienced the best as well as the most challenging seasons living in a glass house. Drawing from life and God's word, she offers encouragement for the journey.

She is an award-winning author of the middle grade series *The Crumberry Chronicles* (*The Wish I Wished Last Night* and *Battle Buddies*) as well as contributing to numerous books and devotions including "The Upper Room," "Power for Living," and "Guidepost Christmas Edition." Her current work in progress is volume 3 in *The Crumberry Chronicles*.

Made in the USA
San Bernardino, CA
04 January 2020

62658469R00102